SUBCOMANDANTE
MARCOS

SUBCOMANDANTE MARCOS

GLOBAL REBEL ICON

NICK HENCK

Montréal • Chicago • London

Black Rose Books No. TT402

Library and Archives Canada Cataloguing in Publication

Title: Subcomandante Marcos: global rebel icon / Nick Henck.
Names: Henck, Nick, 1971- author.
Identifiers: Canadiana (print) 20190079894 | Canadiana (ebook) 20190079908
    | ISBN 9781551647043 (softcover) | ISBN 9781551647029 (hardcover) |
    ISBN 9781551647067 (PDF)
Subjects: LCSH: Marcos, subcomandante. | LCSH: Guerrillas—Mexico—
    Chiapas—Biography. | LCSH: Revolutionaries—Mexico—Chiapas—
    Biography. | LCSH: Mexico—Politics and government—1988-2000. |
    LCSH: Mexico—Politics and government—2000- | LCSH: Ejército Zapatista
    de Liberación Nacional (Mexico) | LCSH: Chiapas (Mexico)—History—
    Peasant Uprising, 1994- | LCGFT: Biographies.
Classification: LCC F1256.M365 H46 2019 | DDC 972/.750836092—dc23

BLACK ROSE BOOKS

C.P.35788 Succ. Léo-Pariseau
Montréal, QC, H2X 0A4
Canada
Explore our books and subscribe to our newsletter:
www.blackrosebooks.com

Ordering Information

USA/INTERNATIONAL	CANADA	UK/EUROPE
University of Chicago Press Chicago Distribution Center 11030 South Langley Avenue Chicago IL 60628	University of Toronto Press 5201 Dufferin Street Toronto, ON M3H 5T8	Central Books 50 Freshwater Road Chadwell Heath, London RM8 1RX
(800) 621-2736 (USA) (773) 702-7000 (International) orders@press.uchicago.edu	1-800-565-9523 utpbooks@utpress.utoronto.ca	+44 (0) 20 8525 8800 contactus@centralbooks.com

Black Rose Books is a not-for-profit publishing project of Cercle Noir et Rouge

To el subcomandante

Everything that makes Power and the good consciences of those in power uncomfortable – this is Marcos.

Subcomandante Marcos

*

Tyrion Lannister:	What is it that you want exactly?
Lord Varys:	Peace. Prosperity. A land where the powerful do not prey on the powerless.
Tyrion Lannister:	…The powerful have always preyed on the powerless, that's how they became powerful in the first place.
Lord Varys:	Perhaps. And perhaps we've grown so used to horror we assume there's no other way.

Game of Thrones

*

Then I come here and hear someone say that our [indigenous] communities are ignorant. I fill my pipe with tobacco, light it, and then say:

> "Damn! What an honour to be able to be a student of so much and such scrumptious ignorance!"

Subcomandante Marcos

TABLE OF CONTENTS

ACKNOWLEDGMENTS

First, I would like to thank the team at *Black Rose Books* for having faith in this project from the outset, as well as for their continued commitment and assistance throughout the entire publication process. Secondly, I owe a heartfelt debt of gratitude to my colleagues in Keio University's Faculty of Law, and especially those in the English Department, for their gracious support and kindness over the last fourteen years—*kore kara mo yoroshiku onegaiitashimasu*. Next, sincere gratitude goes to Ricardo Trabulsi for furnishing me with the photograph that adorns the cover of this book: I believe it captures perfectly not only the iconic aura that attends Subcomandante Marcos but also his profound humanity. Last but by no means least, love and appreciation go to Louis, who teaches me something new each day (even though he is only five), and Yasuko, who has taught me much (and from whom I am sure I could learn even more were I a better listener).

TIME LINE

June 19, 1957

Rafael Guillén, the future Subcomandante Marcos, is born.

September 1977

Rafael enrols in the Faculty of Philosophy and Literature at the country's pre-eminent National Autonomous University of Mexico (UNAM in Spanish) in Mexico City.

January 1979

Rafael begins teaching at Mexico City's prestigious Metropolitan Autonomous University (UAM in Spanish). This year sees him join the ranks of the clandestine revolutionary organization, the Forces of National Liberation (FLN in Spanish).

October 1980

Rafael submits an award-winning graduation thesis to complete his undergraduate studies at UNAM.

August 1984

Rafael, having adopted the *nom de guerre* Marcos, leaves the capital to join the FLN's Chiapas wing, the Zapatista Army of National Liberation (EZLN in Spanish), or "the Zapatistas" for short, as a rural guerrilla.

November 1986	Marcos is promoted to the rank of subcomandante.
January 1, 1994	Marcos makes his debut on the world stage.
February/March 1994	Marcos attends peace talks with the government.
July 1994	*Vanity Fair* publishes a feature on Marcos titled "Mexico's Poet Rebel" that includes an interview with him.
August 1994	Marcos presides over the National Democratic Convention attended by more than 6,000 members of Mexican civil society. Shortly afterwards, the US TV news program *60 Minutes* broadcasts a feature on the Zapatistas that contains an interview with Marcos.
February 1995	Marcos is "unmasked" by President Zedillo who reveals the identity of the Subcomandante.
January 1996	Marcos gives the closing speech at the first ever National Indigenous Forum, which was attended by 500 representatives from more than 30 indigenous groups from all over Mexico.

April/May 1996

Marcos has a succession of meetings with, among others, movie director Oliver Stone; France's former First Lady Danielle Mitterrand; and French intellectual and one-time intimate of Che Guevara, Régis Debray.

July/August 1996

Marcos hosts the Intercontinental Encuentro For Humanity and Against Neoliberalism attended by more than 3,000 participants from more than 50 countries, as well as members of Mexican civil society, and the North American and European media. Marcos grants a book-length interview to French sociologist Yvon Le Bot and has a photo shoot with France's fashion magazine *Marie Claire*.

Spring 1999

La Historia de los Colores / The Story of Colors, a bilingual version of one of Marcos' stories, illustrated with artwork by an indigenous artist, is published in hardcover book form. It sells 6,000 copies in the first 48 hours.

April 1999–February 2000

Marcos enters into numerous exchanges in the national press with various Mexican public intellectuals and academics on the subject of the strike by students at UNAM over tuition fee hikes.

May 1999	Marcos hosts the Zapatistas' Second Encuentro with Civil Society, giving a speech of welcome to the almost 2,000 attendees. It was his first major public appearance in 18 months.
November 1999	Spanish journalist and novelist Manuel Vázquez Montalbán publishes a book-length interview with the Subcomandante titled *Marcos: el señor de los espejos* (*Marcos: Lord of the Mirrors*).
February/March 2001	Marcos heads a Zapatista delegation embarking on a March for Indian Dignity to Mexico City, culminating in a rally held in the capital's central square attended by more than 100,000 people. He is interviewed by, among others, Nobel laureate Gabriel García Márquez.
December 2004	Marcos co-authors *The Uncomfortable Dead* with Mexico's famous detective novelist Paco Ignacio Taibo II.
September 2005	Marcos announces that he will be visiting all of Mexico's states on a six-month tour of the country dubbed The Other Campaign.
January 2006	Marcos sets out on The Other Campaign.

May–October 2006	The Other Campaign is suspended as Marcos decides to remain in and around Mexico City in solidarity with some 200 or more demonstrators who had been beaten and arrested by police in Atenco.
June 2006	Marcos is interviewed by veteran journalist Jesús Quintero on Spain's national public state-owned television channel TVE. More than 1.9 million viewers tune in.
December 2006	The Other Campaign comes to an end. Marcos had succeeded in personally reaching out to and forging links with many among Mexico's marginalized, including its LGBTQ community.
January 2007	Marcos addresses over 2,000 people from 43 countries at The First Encounter between the Zapatistas and the Peoples of the World.
June 2007	Marcos' lavishly illustrated erotic tale entitled *Noches de fuego y desvelo* (*Fiery and Sleepless Nights*) is published.
July 2007	Marcos again addresses more than 2,000 people at The Second

Encounter between the Zapatistas and the Peoples of the World. He also presents three papers: at the National Educational Institute for Anthropological and Historical Studies in Mexico City; at the Press Club, also located in the capital; and lastly at the University of the Earth in San Cristóbal, Chiapas.

October 2007	Marcos delivers a closing speech at The Encuentro of the Indigenous Peoples of America held in Sonora.
November 2007	Marcos grants a book-length interview to Mexican journalist and expert on Mexico's armed Left, Laura Castellanos.
December 2007	Marcos gives a series of seven anti-capitalist presentations at The First International Colloquium in Memory of Andrés Aubry: Planet Earth: Anti-systemic Movements, alongside prominent speakers that include John Berger, Naomi Klein, and Immanuel Wallerstein, and in front of an audience of almost 2,000 attendees from 34 countries.
August 2008	Marcos jointly hosts, along with Lieutenant Colonel Moisés, The National and International

	Caravan for Observation and Solidarity with Zapatista Communities, delivering speeches to over 300 Mexican and foreign solidarity activists and human rights promoters.
January 2009	Marcos delivers a series of five anti-capitalist presentations, alongside an array of other left-wing luminaries, among them noted U.S. political-theorist Michael Hardt, before an audience of 3,500 at The Global Festival of Dignified Rage.
March 2011	Marcos enters into a four-part exchange of letters, through the pages of the Mexican daily *La Jornada*, with distinguished Mexican philosopher Luis Villoro in which they discuss politics and ethics.
2013	Marcos issues a flood of communiqués, including 19 in his *Them and Us* series (January–March), another five in his *Classmates* series (June), four more in his *Votán* series (July and August), and three in his *Rewind* series (November and December).
May 25, 2014	The Subcomandante delivers a speech before several thousand in

which he announces the death of Marcos and his rebirth as Galeano. He is no longer the Zapatistas' sole spokesperson; instead, he now shares this role with a younger, indigenous and recently promoted Subcomandante Moisés.

May 2015	Marcos, now as Galeano, gives two speeches of tribute before an audience of more than 5,000 at The Celebration in Homage to Compañeros Luis Villoro Toranzo and Zapatista Teacher Galeano, and makes seven presentations at the Zapatistas' week-long Seminar on Critical Thought in the Face of the Capitalist Hydra, attended by 2,600 people.
February 2016	The twenty-year statute of limitations on the charges levelled against Marcos by the Mexican government in February 1995 comes to an end.
December 2016–January 2017	Some 82 scientists hailing from over 50 scientific disciplines and 11 countries attend The Zapatistas and ConSciences for Humanity, which sees Subcomandante Galeano deliver four single presentations and two joint ones (with Subcomandante Moisés).

April 2017	Galeano delivers the opening speech, as well as two presentations, at the Zapatista seminar titled The Walls of Capital, the Cracks of the Left.
Summer 2017	Galeano's *Habrá una vez* (*Once Upon a Time*), a collection of stories featuring a young Zapatista girl, is published, as is *Escritos Sobre la Guerra y la Economía Política* (*Writings on War and Political Economy*), a collection of his communiqués and essays that critique capitalism.
May 2017–February 2018	Galeano puts his weight behind María de Jesús Patricio Martínez, or "Marichuy" as she is also known, supporting her bid to become Mexico's first indigenous, female presidential candidate. However, she fails to secure the minimum number of endorsements necessary to run before the deadline expires.
April 2018	Galeano plays a prominent role at the eleven-day event titled Gazes, Harkenings, Words: No Thinking Allowed?, convened by the Zapatistas to discuss how organizing votes for Marichuy's candidacy had further generated autonomous collective

organization; and the up-coming general election in July. He makes 16 presentations, totalling more than six-and-half hours, and participates in roundtable discussions.

INTRODUCTION

Subcomandante Marcos is far better known in the Spanish-speaking world than in the English-speaking one. Moreover, when he is recognized by English-speakers, it is often simply for being the media-savvy spokesperson for a prominent Mexican social movement made up of predominantly indigenous peoples. Marcos is, however, far more than the mere mouthpiece and representative of an indigenous social movement, since while vitally important in that role, he also became the interface between Mexico's rural indigenous communities on the one hand and urban mestizo society (and even global civil society) on the other. The Subcomandante is also, for example: an author of not inconsiderable literary repute; a renovator and revitalizer of the Left's political language; and a champion of not only indigenous peoples (in the face of racism, discrimination and neglect), but also all of Mexico's downtrodden, in particular defending and promoting the rights of such marginalized groups as the LBGTQ community and women. He has been an initiator of positive change in Mexican politics, at the very least by helping to make the country democratic, especially (but not only) by contributing significantly to the ousting of the Institutional Revolutionary Party (PRI in Spanish), which had held power for over seven decades. The Subcomandante is a fierce, highly visible and vocal critic of Mexico's political class; a proponent of radical grass-roots democracy; an advocate of "another way of doing politics"; a political theorist and practitioner (i.e. activist) of considerable note; and a leading luminary in the alter-globalization[1] and anti-capitalist movements. He has also been hailed as an icon (and had the label "iconic" attached to him), as well as having been dubbed a "multicultural hero" and "a legend in his own time." He has even been compared to Gandhi and Nelson Mandela in terms of being a "world moral hero," and to John F. Kennedy in the 1960s as a political figure who enjoys "popularity in virtually all sectors of…society."[2]

The future Subcomandante Marcos began his life as Rafael Sebastián Guillén Vicente, born on June 19, 1957 in Tampico, a port city in the Mexican gulf state of Tamaulipas. The Mexico that Rafael was born into had emerged from the Twentieth century's first revolution (1910–1920) only 40 years earlier. From the wreckage of that decade-long traumatic social convulsion emerged the PRI, which would govern Mexico for the next 70 years. Although the presidency of Lázaro Cárdenas (1934–1940) had seen the implementation of progressive land and labour reforms, for the remainder of the century the PRI would rule largely through a combination of co-optation, coercion, corruption, electoral fraud, and repression, leading Peruvian Nobel laureate Mario Vargas Llosa in 1990 to dub it "the perfect dictatorship." The years and decades following Rafael's birth witnessed major government repression: in 1958–59, the railroad workers were brutally suppressed; in 1968, several hundred students were killed in the Tlatelolco Massacre; in the early and mid-1970s, members of left-wing student and militant groups were tortured, disappeared and assassinated during Mexico's "Dirty War"; and in 1975, the electrical workers' movement was crushed.

Rafael came from a middle-class family, his father owning a small chain of furniture stores in the city, and he was a "middle child," being the fourth of eight offspring. His parents, both of whom had previously worked as teachers, placed a great deal of emphasis on education, with the result that all of the Guillén children went on to attend university, with one of Rafael's brothers, Alfonso, even becoming a professor of Mexican History at South Baja California State University. Thanks to his parents' efforts, Rafael was able to recite lengthy poems even before he could read, and enjoyed considerable exposure to literature and poetry throughout his childhood.[3] This early, profound, and sustained acquaintance with literature would lead, as we shall see in Chapter 2, to Marcos himself becoming an author of some literary repute and to his formulating an innovative, inspiring, and engaging political language. As for Rafael's formal education, he attended Jesuit primary and secondary schools, although he has stated in an interview that in his family "we were very independent of religion. It was a very humanist tradition."[4] Perhaps illustrative of this is the fact that while he took his First Holy Communion aged eight, he appears not to have subsequently undergone Confirmation (which usually takes place at around aged twelve).[5]

After leaving high school in 1977, Rafael moved from provincial Tampico to the country's cosmopolitan capital, Mexico City, enrolling in the prestigious National Autonomous University of Mexico (UNAM in Spanish). According to his father, "Rafael had always liked philosophy, and this is what he wanted to study."[6] It was only natural then that he should choose to enter the university's School of Philosophy and Literature, specializing in political philosophy, especially that belonging to the contemporary French School. In particular, he appears to have been influenced profoundly and lastingly by three thinkers: the structural Marxists, Louis Althusser and Nicos Poulantzas, and the post-structural, post-Marxist, Michel Foucault. His award-winning graduation thesis drew heavily on these philosophers' works.

It was also while at university that he made contact with, and joined the ranks of, the Forces of National Liberation (FLN in Spanish), a clandestine Marxist-Leninist revolutionary organization whose self-declared aim was "the taking of political power for the peasants and the workers of the Mexican Republic, to establish a popular republic with a socialist system."[7] The FLN—especially its leadership—were heavily inspired by the Cuban Revolution (1959), and in particular the figure of Che Guevara, which may help explain why Rafael was drawn to the organization, having hero-worshipped Guevara from his youth.[8] As for its composition, Marcos tells us, "The majority of the [FLN's] members…were from the middle class; university professors, professionals, engineers, medics," adding that "It was a very, very small group: I am talking of ten or so, perhaps twenty people."[9] Despite being few in number, the FLN's members were extremely committed and no doubt experienced a further boosting of morale and strengthening of their revolutionary convictions as a result of the Sandinistas' sweeping to power in Nicaragua (1979) in Latin America's second (after Cuba in 1959) successful Left-wing Revolution. Significantly however, the FLN was considerably less doctrinaire or dogmatic and far more eclectic or ideologically heterogeneous than was typical of Latin American left-wing revolutionary organizations of the time.[10]

The five years from 1979–1984 saw Rafael, then aged 22–27, graduate from UNAM, take up a teaching post at the capital's highly acclaimed and somewhat radical Metropolitan Autonomous University (UAM in Spanish), and assume increasing responsibilities and duties within the FLN under the pseudonym "Zacarías." Also during this period, there is evidence to suggest that he visited Nicaragua, the scene of the recent Sandinista revolution (1979). We know for certain that he frequently went to Mexico's South-Eastern state of Chiapas, where the FLN had local contacts, to meet these and to undergo rural guerrilla training.

On August 6, 1984, the 15th anniversary of the founding of the FLN, Rafael—swapping the nom de guerre "Zacarías" for that of "Marcos" (the name of a recently fallen comrade)—left Mexico City to permanently embark on rural guerrilla life as part of the FLN's recently established wing in Chiapas, called the Zapatista Army of National Liberation (EZLN in Spanish). While Chiapas was chosen as the base from which to launch a guerrilla insurrection because of its geographical isolation, and also because the FLN had contacts in the area from a previous failed attempt to establish a guerrilla group there, the state's socio-economic and political landscape helped make it fertile ground for rebellion. Many of Chiapas' indigenous peasants were mired in grinding poverty and endured chronic neglect or even brutal exploitation. Political exclusion and disenfranchisement were rife, and even when indigenous peasants did manage to participate in voting, electoral fraud ensured their votes did not count. Time and again, attempts by peasants to organize themselves were met with severe repression, with members of independent [i.e. non-government affiliated] organizations suffering assassination, disappearance, kidnapping, jailing, torture, and intimidation. So too, peaceful protest marches were fired upon by state security forces, who were also deployed on occasion to expel peasant families from their homes and even level indigenous communities to the ground.[11]

In the early days, the EZLN was a very small guerrilla nucleus, moving clandestinely throughout the Chiapan hinterland and making contact with indigenous communities in order to build up a support base. Over the next few years, Marcos rapidly rose through the EZLN's ranks to jointly head the guerrilla group along with fellow subcomandantes Pedro and Daniel. During the same period, the guerrillas' rank-and-file numbers steadily swelled, until the organization experienced an explosion in the number of local recruits in the late 1980s and early 1990s thanks to a combination of: at the local level, exploitation, racism and repression; at the national level, electoral fraud and impoverishing neoliberal economic policies implemented in preparation for Mexico's entrance into NAFTA; and at the global level, a drastic drop in the price of coffee, the main cash crop cultivated by indigenous peasants.[12]

By 1993 the EZLN had reached a critical juncture. Marcos tells us that the indigenous who constituted the overwhelming majority of the Zapatistas' ranks and support base believed they were facing an existential dilemma. They could either rise up, risking personal loss of life, so as to draw attention to the death of indigenous people—15,000 of whom in Chiapas alone were dying each year from perfectly curable diseases, with many others dying from malnutrition—or carry on as usual, surviving on an individual basis but confronting the very real prospect of dying out as indigenous peoples.[13] Ultimately, the Zapatistas chose both to utilize the momentum they had built up on account of the recent massive swelling of their ranks, and to seize the opportunity afforded by the coming into effect of NAFTA on January 1, 1994, to rise up and make their voices heard.[14]

With Subcomandante Daniel having quit the EZLN in the run up to the uprising, and with Subcomandante Pedro being shot dead during the Zapatistas' opening assault, Marcos emerged as the sole military leader of the movement. At the same time, with the Zapatistas garnering considerable media attention and significant public support through their rebellion, Marcos was able to secure the EZLN's autonomy and independence from its mother organization, the FLN. The Subcomandante would spend the next two decades (1994–2014) in Chiapas acting as the Zapatistas' chief military advisor and spokesperson, before taking more of a back seat to make way for a younger and (for the first time in the EZLN's history) indigenous subcomandante, Moisés, to come to the fore. In May 2014 Subcomandante Marcos publicly announced that he would hitherto cease to exist: then and there he re-baptised himself Subcomandante Galeano, and in doing so assumed his most recent incarnation to date. In the years since, he has continued to author Zapatista communiqués, and to attend, participate in, and even host Zapatista events, although he now tends to share these duties with Subcomandante Moisés.

CHAPTER 1

SUBCOMANDANTE AND
SPOKESPERSON

With Marcos having been the Zapatistas' high-profile spokesperson for nearly a quarter-of-a-century, it is easy to forget that initially his role within the organization had been that of a guerrilla leader. He, and two other subcomandantes, Daniel and Pedro, were each in charge of a base camp complete with several hundred troops and a local zone of influence. Marcos' duties included being responsible for local recruitment, and then carrying out the political education and consciousness raising, as well as the military training, of these raw recruits. No doubt too, he, in conjunction with Subcomandante Pedro—Subcomandante Daniel having quit the organization six months before the uprising—masterminded the military operations, which included the takeover of several towns and an assault on an army base during the January 1, 1994 rebellion. Furthermore, with Subcomandante Pedro's sudden death in battle on the first day of the uprising, we must also suppose that it was left to Marcos to co-ordinate and effect the timely and orderly retreat in the face of the Federal Army's push-back, which he did fairly successfully given the situation. Almost a year later, in December 1994, Marcos also masterminded a massive but non-violent manoeuvre which involved the Zapatistas breaking the encirclement of their territory by slipping through Army lines and occupying town halls and highways.

This military stage in the Zapatista movement's development, which Marcos presided over, was a crucial one, as the Subcomandante, looking back, himself makes clear:

> It would be naïve to think that all the good things we have accomplished—including the privilege of listening to and learning from you—would have been possible without preparing a full decade for the sun to rise as it rose on 1 January, 15 years ago.[15]

> We did not make ourselves known with a march or a "we-the-undersigned" document. We made ourselves known to the world with an army, with battles against the federal troops, with armed resistance... you met us at war.[16]

Elsewhere, Marcos asserts:

> Nothing that we have done, for better or for worse, would have been possible if an army, the Zapatista Army of National Liberation, had not risen up against the evil government exercising the right to legitimate violence: the violence of those below against the violence of those above.[17]

Following nearly a fortnight of fighting, a ceasefire ordered by the president of Mexico on January 12, 1994 issued-in a major shift in the nature of Marcos' main role within the Zapatista movement. Although the Zapatistas retained their arms, both to deter the threat of a resumption of hostilities by the Mexican Army and to use as leverage in negotiations with the government, the Subcomandante's primary function would henceforth be that of the movement's spokesperson, which encompassed the duties of press officer, PR man, front-man or headliner, and cultural translator or conduit between the two estranged entities that were

Chiapas' indigenous people and the wider world. This role, which was vital for the movement's very survival—since ensuring that it remained in the media spotlight would forestall any attempt by the Mexican government to employ a military solution in dealing with the Zapatistas—was one that Marcos would perform masterfully for more than two decades. In sum, in his capacity as military leader, the Subcomandante had succeeded in turning the world's gaze toward the Zapatistas' through orchestrating their armed rebellion, but it was through acting as the movement's spokesperson that he would subsequently sustain this attention.

On the first day of the uprising, in San Cristóbal, the largest town that the Zapatistas seized, Marcos delivered a speech from the town hall balcony addressing citizens who had assembled there, gave four interviews, and spoke to tourists allaying their concerns regarding safety and planned travel schedules. In both his address and all four interviews the Subcomandante stressed that the uprising was one that was being carried out by indigenous peoples who were rebelling against the appalling conditions and treatment that they were forced to endure.

The months, years, and decades that followed the 1994 uprising saw Marcos dedicating himself to raising the public profile of the movement, garnering national and international support for it, publicizing its plight by outlining its experiences, and promoting its thinking and practices. This he did through issuing communiqués, giving interviews, holding press conferences, touring the country and giving speeches at stops on the way, meeting with high-profile personalities, and fronting national and international gatherings. The first three months of 1994, for example, saw the Subcomandante penning over 60 communiqués, giving 24 interviews (i.e. an average of two a week); and participating in ten days of peace negotiations with the government, during which he also held nine press conferences reporting on the progress being made and dashed off several communiqués.

Marcos' output of communiqués has been voluminous. He issued almost 100 in the first six months of the uprising (i.e. an average one every two days), and had notched up some 360 by the end of 1997. Moreover, a compilation of his communiqués, plus the Subcomandante's speeches (but excluding any interviews), covering the first seven years and three months (i.e. January 1994–April 2001) of the post-uprising period, comprises five volumes totalling over 1900 closely-typed pages.[18] Nor, frequently, did these communiqués take the form of terse statements typical of this means of communication; instead, they were often quite considerable in length. For instance, *Our Word is Our Weapon*, which collects and translates a hundred communiqués, totals over 400 pages, while another English-language edited collection, ¡Ya Basta! *Ten Years of the Zapatista Uprising*, contains 130 communiqués and totals 628 pages, to give an average page length of about 4.5 pages per document. In some instances, Marcos' communiqués formed a series of protracted, detailed and markedly involved exchanges. There is, for example, his correspondence with leading Mexican literary figure Carlos Monsiváis and certain academics regarding the year-long strike at the National Autonomous University of Mexico (1999–2000), as well as his four-part "dialogue" with eminent philosopher Luis Villoro in which the two men discussed at length politics and ethics (2011). So too, in 2013 alone the Subcomandante issued a flood of communiqués: 19 in his *Them and Us* series (January to March), another five in his *Classmates* series (June), four more in his *Votán* series (July and August), and three in his *Rewind* series (November and December).

Viewed as a corpus, these writings constitute the vehicle by means of which Marcos: disseminated the Zapatistas' political program and promoted their core values (e.g. demanding democracy, social justice, and respect for indigenous rights and culture, as well as an end to both neoliberal economic policies and discrimination against women and members of the LGBTQ community); countered the government's anti-Zapatista propaganda, especially its portrayal of the Zapatistas as "professionals of violence" (as President Salinas had labelled them); announced upcoming Zapatista events, such as mobilizations, marches, press conferences, gatherings and so on, and invited high-profile figures to attend these; established contact, and even expressed solidarity, with other likeminded or similarly oppressed individuals, peoples and organizations; addressed, responded to and rebutted allegations made by critics; critiqued government policies; exposed the hypocrisy of the ruling elite; publicized infractions of the ceasefire on the part of the Mexican military, or intimidation, threats and attacks by paramilitaries; challenged both the Government's dominant discourse and the press' portrayal of events; lampooned the powerful, and in particular the political, social and economic elite; and finally, championed, and gave voice to, the poor and oppressed. In this sense, his use of communiqués renders Marcos a modern-day pamphleteer.

The Subcomandante was also a master of the interview. In the first six months of 1994 alone he notched up forty, and he has given dozens since, some of them of book length. Marcos' interlocutors would include eminent literary figures (e.g. Gabriel García Márquez, Manuel Vázquez Montalbán, Juan Gelman, Carlos Monsiváis, Elena Poniatowska, and Guadalupe Loaeza); reporters from major news organizations, both national (e.g. the Mexican dailies *La Jornada*, *Reforma*, *Excélsior*, and *El Financiero*, and the political weekly magazine *Proceso*) and international (e.g. *60 Minutes*, *The New York Times*, *The Miami Herald*, *The Associated Press*, *Noticiero Univision*, and *Cambio*); newspaper and news magazine editors (such as *Le Monde diplomatique*'s Ignacio Ramonet and *Proceso*'s Julio Scherer); academics such as the sociologists Marta Durán de Huerta (from Mexico) and Yvon Le Bot (from France); documentary film-makers (e.g. Cristián Calónico, Nicholas P. Higgins, and Saul Landau); and correspondents for lifestyle magazines (e.g. *Vanity Fair* and *Marie Claire*). As an example, between January 8 and March 25, 2001 Marcos gave more than ten interviews, and in the 17-month period between May 2006 and November 2007, he gave another succession of interviews, several of which were substantial (two were long enough to be published in short book form), and one of which was broadcast on Spanish television.[19] Marcos also invited numerous prominent personalities to meet and talk with him and, although some declined, others grasped the opportunity. Oliver Stone, the acclaimed US movie director; Danielle Mitterrand, wife of the former French President, François Mitterrand; and Régis Debray (the French intellectual who had visited Che Guevara in his guerrilla camp during his ill-fated Bolivian campaign and who had also acted as an advisor to President Mitterrand); all trekked into the jungle to converse with the Subcomandante. These meetings were then reported in the world affairs section of an edition of *Newsweek*, appearing in a piece titled "The Return of Guerrilla Chic" that carried photographs of Stone shaking hands with Marcos, and Mitterrand standing alongside several Zapatistas.[20]

Marcos also orchestrated and headed two major Zapatista tours. The first was their 2001 caravan which toured 13 states of the nation in a little over two weeks (February 24–March 11), culminating in a mass rally held in the capital's main square attended by over 100,000 (and perhaps as many as double that) supporters. The caravan, which paused in 33 communities along its 3,000 km journey, saw Marcos give 22 speeches in 16 days, delivering two per day on five days, three in one day, and only having one day when he gave none at all. Furthermore, after the caravan arrived in Mexico City, the Subcomandante, despite having only just completed this gruelling speech-packed schedule, immediately began delivering more speeches, and giving numerous interviews. An insight into his intense activity at that time can be seen from his schedule while in the capital. Arriving at the city's outskirts in the afternoon of March 8th, he gave a speech the following day in Milpa Alta; granted a 75-minute interview with renowned author, journalist, editor, and founder of *Proceso*, Julio Scherer at 2 a.m. on the 10th, and spoke publicly the same day in Xochimilco. The next day he gave a speech in the capital's main plaza; and on the 12th, he gave a speech at the Olympic Village convened by the National School of Anthropology and History and attended by literary luminaries such as Nobel laureate José Saramago, Spanish detective novelist Manuel Vázquez Montálban, and Mexico's leading authors Carlos Monsiváis, Carlos Montemayor, and Elena Poniatowska, as well as award-winning sociologists Pablo González Casanova (from Mexico) and Alain Touraine (from France). On March 13, he gave a brief press conference and, after a day's break, he resumed with characteristic intensity. On the 15th he gave two separate interviews with Uruguay's *The Spectator* and *The Observer*; the next day he spoke at the National Polytechnic Institute, one of the nation's largest public universities; and on the 18th he spoke first at the National School of Anthropology and History, and afterwards to children in the Isidro Fabela neighbourhood where the School is situated. On the 20th he gave short speeches at each of the Metropolitan Autonomous University's three campuses to a combined total of 12,000 students, academics and university workers; and the following day he delivered a speech at the National Autonomous University of Mexico to a crowd estimated at 60,000. Finally, on the 22nd he spoke at a rally in front of the Saint Lazarus Legislative Palace, where the Chamber of Deputies meets. Indeed, when asked on the tour by one interviewer "What's your average day like just now?" the Subcomandante quipped "I get up, I give interviews and then it's time to go to bed."[21]

The second tour took place in 2006 and was called The Other Campaign. It represented both an alternative to the presidential campaign then being conducted by Mexico's main political parties and also an attempt, as the Zapatistas themselves explained, "to listen to and talk directly…with the simple and humble people of Mexico and…to build…a national platform of struggle…that is clearly left-wing i.e. anticapitalist, i.e. anti-neoliberal, i.e. in favour of justice, democracy, and freedom for the Mexican people."[22] In contrast to the 2001 tour, which had seen Marcos and 23 Zapatista Commanders travelling much of the nation in a large bus and holding mass rallies along the way, all in the full glare of the media spotlight, The Other Campaign was more low key. And, whereas the 2001 tour had sought to gain popular support for indigenous rights, this 2006 one aimed at forging a coalition of all of Mexico's downtrodden, with Marcos reaching out personally to thousands of the nation's marginalized while affording them a chance to voice their grievances and have these heard. It primarily involved the Subcomandante traversing the country largely as a one-man show, spending his time in comparatively small gatherings (of tens or hundreds as opposed to thousands). Typically, he would listen at length to local people describing their daily struggle against exploitation, after which he would speak, briefly identifying the common sources of, and means employed in, their oppression, drawing parallels between their maltreatment and their resistance to it, and similar experiences on the part of indigenous people in general, and Zapatista communities in Chiapas in particular. Even on this tour however, there were opportunities for the Subcomandante to give speeches to sizable crowds, usually when he passed through large cities or towns, as happened when he addressed several thousand people who had gathered to hear him in the central plaza of the state capital Oaxaca.

Marcos also gave speeches in his capacity as master of ceremonies (of sorts) at the numerous events that the Zapatistas organized. The Subcomandante acted as host, for example, at the August 1994 National Democratic Convention which took place just before the presidential elections that year. The event, which appears to have been the brainchild of Marcos, aimed at bringing together various sectors of civil society in order, as the Subcomandante put it, "to debate and agree on the organisation of a civil, peaceful, popular and national struggle for democracy, freedom and justice."[23] The Convention was attended by 6,000 participants and included members of both national and international organizations, hundreds of individuals who were

Zapatista sympathizers, key Mexican progressive luminaries such as Elena Poniatowska and Carlos Monsiváis (both of whom published detailed accounts extolling the event's importance), and 711 journalists from 400 national and international news organizations. The Subcomandante's welcome speech—in which he likened the event to Noah's Ark, the Tower of Babel, and Fitzcarraldo's steamship in the jungle—reiterated the Zapatistas' famous motto and guiding principle of "for everyone, everything; nothing for ourselves." It ended with the Subcomandante dramatically unfurling the Mexican flag and declaring "...the EZLN now gives you the national flag in order to remind you of what it means: Country, History and Nation. And we commit ourselves to that which it ought to mean: Democracy, Freedom, Justice."[24] The speech drew rapturous applause.

1996 in particular proved an especially busy year for the Subcomandante in terms of hosting events at which he also gave speeches. In January, he delivered the closing speech at the National Indigenous Forum. In April, he gave the opening and closing speeches to the American Preparatory Meeting for the Intercontinental Gathering For Humanity and Against Neoliberalism, also delivering a presentation during that three-day event. Finally, at the end of July and beginning of August, Marcos presided over and gave the closing speech at the Intercontinental Gathering For Humanity and Against Neoliberalism. The event saw between 4,000 and 5,000 attendees, many of them representatives of various leftist organizations and social movements, hailing from around 50 countries, trek into Zapatista territory for the gathering. Accompanying them was a veritable host of press intent on covering the event, as well as two documentary film crews who incorporated footage from the gathering into their works, *A Place Called Chiapas* (1998) and *Zapatista* (1999). In addition to acting as the event's host, on the side-lines Marcos also participated in a photo shoot for the French edition of the leading fashion magazine *Marie Claire* and granted a book-length interview to esteemed French sociologist

Yvon Le Bot. The Intercontinental thus proved a major public relations coup.

The years that followed saw other notable instances of the Subcomandante giving speeches while hosting major Zapatista events. For example, at the Second National Gathering of Civil Society (May 1999), Marcos delivered a speech addressed to an audience of 2,000. So too, he gave addresses in front of over 2,000 attendees at both The First Encounter between the Zapatistas and the Peoples of the World and The Second Encounter between the Zapatistas and the Peoples of the World (January and July 2007, respectively). He also jointly hosted, along with Lieutenant Colonel Moisés, the National and International Caravan for Observation and Solidarity with Zapatista Communities (August 2008), in which both men delivered speeches to over 300 Mexican and foreign solidarity activists and human rights promoters who had travelled to Chiapas to see the challenges facing Zapatista communities and the innovative solutions the latter were devising and implementing in response to these. In 2014, only hours after a gathering to pay homage to murdered Zapatista support-base member and teacher "Galeano," Marcos delivered a speech before the more than 2,000 support-base members, 600 solidarity supporters, as well as numerous members of the alternative press, who had attended the preceding gathering, in which he announced his on-the-spot transformation from Marcos to Galeano (May 25).[25] The Subcomandante (now as Galeano) also gave two speeches of tribute before an audience of more than 5,000 at The Celebration in Homage to Compañeros Luis Villoro Toranzo and Zapatista Teacher Galeano (May 2015), which he again co-hosted with the recently promoted Subcomandante Moisés. Finally, in April 2017, Galeano delivered the opening speech at The Walls of Capital, the Cracks of the Left seminar.[26]

Indeed, over the last ten years Marcos has played a prominent role in, and delivered substantial presentations at, numerous events convened by the Zapatistas. For example, he presented three papers between July 16 and 19, 2007, first at the National

Educational Institute for Anthropological and Historical Studies in Mexico City, then at the Press Club in the capital, and finally at the Indigenous Centre for Integral Training (University of the Earth) in San Cristóbal, Chiapas. In December 2007, he gave a series of seven presentations at The First International Colloquium in Memory of Andrés Aubry: Planet Earth, Anti-systemic Movements in honour of the French-born ethno-sociologist and historian.[27] There the Subcomandante delivered possibly his most explicit and elaborate critique of capitalism to date, alongside prominent fellow speakers that included the art critic, novelist, painter, and poet, John Berger; award-winning writer, journalist, filmmaker, and activist, Naomi Klein; and world-renowned sociologist Immanuel Wallerstein; and in front of an audience of almost 2,000 attendees from 34 countries. Then, just over a year later, the Zapatistas convened The Global Festival of Dignified Rage, with its theme of "Another World, Another Path: Below and to the Left," the third stage of which (January 2–5, 2009) involved the Subcomandante once more delivering a series of anti-capitalist presentations, again alongside an array of other left-wing luminaries, among them noted U.S. political-theorist Michael Hardt, before an audience of 3,500.[28] So too, at the Seminar on Critical Thought in the Face of the Capitalist Hydra (May 2015), which lasted a week and was attended by 2,600 people, Marcos (now re-baptized Galeano) gave seven presentations, alongside Subcomandante Moisés who made a further seven of his own, not only analyzing and critiquing capitalism but also proposing ways to confront it.[29] Similarly, in the winter of 2016–2017, at The Zapatistas and ConSciences for Humanity (December 26–January 4), in which 82 scientists spanning over 50 scientific disciplines and eleven countries participated, Subcomandante Galeano gave four single presentations and two joint ones (with Subcomandante Moisés) rounding off six of the eight daily general sessions.[30] More recently, Subcomandante Galeano delivered two presentations at the Zapatista-convened seminar titled The Walls of Capital, the Cracks of the Left (April 12–15,

2017).[31] Finally, and most recently, Galeano played a prominent role in the eleven-day long roundtable discussion event organized by the Zapatistas titled Gazes, Harkenings, Words: No Thinking Allowed? (April 15–25, 2018) held at the Indigenous Centre for Integral Training (University of the Earth) in San Cristóbal, Chiapas.[32] The Subcomandante made 16 presentations, totalling more than six-and-a-half hours, and engaged in panel discussions with fellow speakers, who included other members of the Zapatista command, the National Indigenous Congress, and the Indigenous Governing Council, as well as artists, intellectuals, writers, political activists, human rights workers, journalists, and filmmakers.

The Subcomandante has also acted on occasion as the Zapatistas' ambassador at events held by other organizations, and this generally involved him giving speeches expressing solidarity with and offering support to his hosts, as well as outlining the Zapatista movement's position on shared issues. Hence we find the Subcomandante sending, in the form of a video, a 90-minute presentation to the National Democratic Convention in Mexico City (August 1995) and a 10-minute video message to the "Freeing the Media" Independent Media Teach-in that took place in New York (January 1997); giving a presentation at an intercultural gathering of intellectuals at the Mexican capital's National School of Anthropology and History on "Paths of Dignity: Indigenous Rights, Memory and Cultural Heritage" (March 2001); and delivering a speech at the Gathering of the Indigenous Peoples of America, in Vícam, Sonora State (October 2007). The most significant instance however was undoubtedly Marcos' participation in the Third Indigenous Congress (March 2001) at Nurio in Michoacán State. There, as Gary H. Gossen notes,

> representatives from dozens of Mexico's diverse native-language communities voted to make the Zapatistas the "official voice" of the nation's ten to

> fifteen million indigenous people...[and]...Indian
> representatives presented.... Subcomandante Marcos
> with the symbolic staff of indigenous political
> authority to serve as their spokesman.[33]

It is reasonable to suppose that as well as fronting major Zapatista PR events, the Subcomandante was also instrumental in orchestrating them, and may even have masterminded them. The same may well be true of other major undertakings by the Zapatistas that were designed to generate publicity for, and ultimately promote, their cause. If so, the following may also have been the Subcomandante's brainchild: the September 1997 "March" to Mexico City of 1,111 Zapatistas—one for each of the Indigenous communities supporting the movement—that was greeted at its destination by a crowd of tens of thousands;[34] the first Zapatista Consulta (August 1995), which involved a massive (1.3 million responses were garnered) canvassing of national and international public opinion on how to bring about peace and democracy in Chiapas as well as what future path the Zapatistas should take politically; and a second Consulta (March 1999), this time dealing with the issues of indigenous rights and culture (in addition to those of peace and democracy), to which 2.9 million people responded. In any case, even if he was not the sole architect of these events, Marcos was certainly indispensable in organizing, publicizing, promoting, and attracting participants to them.

The Subcomandante was then a highly effective spokesperson and PR publicist for the Zapatista movement. However, his importance proved more profound than this and extended to his functioning as a translator or cultural conduit between two entirely estranged entities: Mexico's rural indigenous peoples and its urban *mestizo* society.[35] It was largely through the medium of Marcos, who has (as Régis Debray puts it) "one foot in the camp of the long-term Indian struggle, the other in that of the hurrying people of the metropolis,"[36] that these two Mexicos began to engage and interact with one another. Prior to Marcos, mainstream Mexican society tended to ignore, and therefore had remained largely ignorant of, the indigenous peoples living alongside it.

Indeed, one of Marcos' greatest achievements was that he managed to move indigenous peoples from the periphery of *mestizo* society's field of vision and place them at the very centre of its gaze. This he managed by, for example, rewriting Mexico's indigenous peoples into the nation's "official history," which until that point had typically excluded, or at the very least grossly marginalized, them. As the Subcomandante pointed out to renowned Mexican journalist Julio Scherer García: "Mexico has had almost 200 years as an independent nation, and at every point in time the indigenous have appeared as the fundamental part, but at no time has any such thing been recognized."[37] This the Subcomandante repeatedly strove to rectify through his communiqués, speeches, presentations, and interviews. In doing so, Marcos succeeded in coaxing Mexican society into recognizing, acknowledging, and accepting the indigenous component of its historical and contemporary social, political, and cultural make-up. He thus ensured that Mexico's national identity would henceforth be partly indigenous and no longer purely *mestizo*. The result, as renowned historian, essayist, literary critic, and public intellectual Enrique Krauze observes, is that "Mexico is different today… more sensitive to the condition of the Indians. That newfound sensitivity is due, in large measure, to the…flamboyant passage (and performance) of Subcomandante Marcos across the stage of history."[38] Most crucially however, the Subcomandante succeeded in placing the issues of indigenous rights and autonomy squarely on the national political agenda, forcing the government to discuss and debate these, to include them in policy decisions, and even to formulate legislation addressing them.

The Subcomandante's adroit and skilled performance in the role of spokesperson and publicist for the Zapatista movement had another important impact on Mexican society: it stimulated intellectual discussion and academic debate in the mass media.

During the first days and weeks of the uprising in January 1994, a good many of Mexico's public intellectuals published pieces in national newspapers corroborating the legitimacy of the Zapatistas' grievances and urging the justice of their demands (though not necessarily their methods, i.e. armed insurrection). By doing so, they proved lifesavers since they ensured the survival of the Zapatistas by helping to shape public opinion in favour of the rebels and by exerting pressure on the government to disavow a policy of military annihilation.

Having witnessed first-hand their effectiveness in acting as "opinion leaders" and "influencers of public opinion and civil society,"[39] Marcos would, over the months and years that followed, devote considerable time and energy to engaging and interacting with numerous high-profile public intellectuals both in Mexico (e.g. Germán Dehesa, Carlos Fuentes, Adolfo Gilly, Pablo González Casanova, Enrique Krauze, Guadalupe Loaeza, Carlos Monsiváis, Elena Poniatowska, Luis Villoro, and Octavio Rodríguez Araujo) and abroad (e.g. John Berger, Eduardo Galeano, Gabriel García Márquez, Eric Jauffret, Naomi Klein, José Saramago, and Manuel Vázquez Montalbán). Some he met with or granted interviews to, others he invited to attend Zapatista conventions and gatherings, and several he called on to act as advisors in the Zapatistas' negotiations with the government. Most typically, however, he would interact with these intellectuals in the pages of national newspapers, entering into correspondence with them through means of communiqués and letters. In some instances, the Subcomandante would respond to a recent piece penned by a particular intellectual that had appeared in the press; at other times he would comment on books which certain public intellectuals had presented him. He would also frequently enter into discussion with them not only on matters pertaining to the Zapatistas, or more broadly to Chiapas or indigenous peoples in general, but also on seemingly unrelated themes such as the 1999–2000 strike at the National Autonomous University of Mexico and other topical issues.

Significantly, even though several of these public intellectuals have expressed their strong disagreement with the Subcomandante in their debates with him on certain issues—with some, as a result, distancing themselves temporarily or sometimes permanently from his standpoint or even his person—the fact remains that they clearly deemed Marcos to be a fellow shaper of public opinion whose writings were worth reading and responding to, and who was himself worth engaging with intellectually.

Perhaps somewhat inevitably, Marcos' intense activity in attracting media attention in the service of the Zapatista cause ultimately led to a considerable cult of personality attaching itself to him. Marcos was quick to recognize this and acknowledge it as something that was far from healthy. Less than a year into the uprising, in November 1994, he gave a speech in which he acknowledged "the protagonistic excesses of he who is the voice of the EZLN"; and six months later, in May 1995, he conceded that "The need for a translator between the indigenous Zapatista culture and the national and international culture caused the obvious nose [i.e. the Subcomandante]…to talk and to write…to an excess…and at times, it seemed to many that the EZLN was only this very visible nose."[40] (In 2008, Marcos would go further, telling a journalist: "If there's anything that I would go back and do differently, it would be to play a less protagonistic role in the media."[41]) However, he was faced with the dilemma that if he retreated from the limelight in order to diminish what several observers dubbed "Marcos-mania,"[42] he risked the movement fading from public view, leaving it vulnerable to renewed attack by the government or paramilitary forces. That this outcome was a likely prospect is borne out by Marcos' observation that the communiqués he authors receive far greater attention and enjoy a much wider circulation than those issued by other Zapatista officers or officials.[43] In this way, the Subcomandante's high public profile became inextricably intertwined with the Zapatista movement's exposure in the media.

The cult of personality that surrounded Marcos was in part fuelled by the romantic appeal of a mysterious rebel located on society's (and the law's) fringes who protects the weak and indigent and who fights against entrenched privilege and abuse of power.[44] Significantly, Marcos has been likened to England's medieval champion of the poor and oppressed, Robin Hood, and Mexico's other masked defender of the downtrodden, Zorro. Added to this, however, were Marcos' own personal qualities; namely, his considerable charisma, charm, wit and eloquence, coupled with his talent for showmanship, theatricality, and sense of occasion.

Indeed, so great was the Subcomandante's appeal that even when, in February 1995, the Mexican government revealed Marcos' true identity, this did not dent his popularity or diminish his appeal. Try as the Government might to portray him as a "professional of violence," the picture of Marcos that ultimately emerged was that of a decent, likable, intelligent, well-educated man from a fairly typical, large, law-abiding, God-fearing, middleclass provincial family who had chosen to abandon a comparatively comfortable life in academia in favour of enduring the hardships of a rural guerrilla existence, living alongside and striving to improve the plight of impoverished and oppressed indigenous peasants.

Even his decision to rise up in arms against the Mexican government did not appear to reduce his standing in many people's eyes, especially since the ruling party had been in power for over seven decades; its most recent president, Salinas, was suspected of having won the presidency through electoral fraud; and the regime itself was widely perceived to be illegitimate, corrupt, and authoritarian. Furthermore, while some disagreed with the Subcomandante's methods, few disputed the justness of the cause he espoused given the patent legitimacy of the grievances vented by Chiapas' indigenous peasants. And so, when civil society mobilized to call a halt to the government's attempts to arrest the Subcomandante following its "unmasking" of him, many marched through the capital's streets chanting the slogan: "We are all Marcos."

The Subcomandante, to his credit, ultimately took decisive action to rectify the over-concentration of attention on him, taking responsibility for having fuelled this phenomenon and expressing his discomfort with it. On May 25, 2014, he gave a public address in which he noted how he had gone "from being a spokesperson to being a distractor" and so had taken the decision to kill off "the character named 'Marcos'" and to adopt a new persona, that of Subcomandante Galeano. In the process of doing so, he was in effect giving up his position as the Zapatistas' sole spokesperson, electing instead henceforth to share this role with a recently appointed younger, indigenous subcomandante, Moisés. Poignantly, in his farewell speech announcing the death of Marcos and the birth of Galeano, the Subcomandante criticized the fixation on him that had taken place in some quarters and pointedly emphasized the importance of collective struggle over that of any one individual.

And yet, it can scarcely be denied that the Zapatista movement had benefited immensely from having had such a charismatic spokesperson and conduit in Marcos. At the very least, we can say that without him the Zapatistas would never have made such a dramatic impact on the national and international stage. Others have gone further, with Alma Guillermoprieto, who, writing just over a year into the Zapatista rebellion, going so far as to suggest that there "was a very real sense in which, during the past thirteen months, *Marcos* fought the Zapatista war single-handed," adding it "was, after all, a public relations war, and the Indian fighters…were not equipped for the sophisticated exchanges with the government and the Mexican public that such a war required."[45] Certainly, through his communiqués, speeches, and interviews Marcos drew political figures, movie directors, literati, intellectuals, artists, academics, journalists, rock musicians, and countless citizens from all over the world not just to the Zapatista banner, but to Chiapas itself, to meet the iconic

Subcomandante and, more significantly in the long run, allow them to see for themselves both the appalling conditions in which Chiapas' indigenous peoples have to live and the innovative and resourceful ways they organize to overcome these deprivations. Moreover, his various *coups de théâtre* served not merely to garner attention for the Zapatista movement and help it forge links and build solidarity with individuals, groups, and organizations worldwide, but also to publicize the daily struggle of indigenous peoples' against discrimination and instil respect toward their way of life, their cosmovision, their beliefs, and their practices.

CHAPTER 2

LITERATURE AND LANGUAGE

In addition to furnishing him with a lifelong love of reading literature, the Subcomandante's extensive and profound exposure to prose and poetry from a young and highly impressionable age resulted in his both becoming an author of some literary repute and devising an innovative, inspiring, and engaging political discourse.

That Marcos is considered an accomplished literary figure in his own right can be seen from the following epithets that have been attached to him: "the best Latin American writer today," a "prominent figure of Mexican letters," "an essayist of the first order," and "a revolutionary Renaissance man...an essayist and raconteur."[46] Moreover, as Jeff Conant points out, he has also been nominated for several literary awards, including "for the Premio Chiapas de Literatura (by noted Chiapanecan poets José Emilio Pacheco, Juan Bañuelos and Óscar Oliva), and for the Premio Chiapas en Arte, with support from esteemed literary figures such as Eduardo Galeano, Elena Poniatowska, and José Emilio Pacheco, among others."[47] Acclaimed essayist and cultural critic Ilan Stavans even selected one of the Subcomandante's works for inclusion in *The Oxford Book of Latin American Essays*. Marcos' literary output is impressive also in terms of the variety of forms it embraces. In addition to hundreds of communiqués, he has published several books, including: two containing parables which take the form of tales from indigenous folklore (*The Story of Colors* and *Questions and Swords*); a clothbound, lavishly illustrated erotic tale (*Fiery and Sleepless Nights*); a detective novel co-written with Paco Ignacio Taibo II (*The Uncomfortable Dead* or *The Inconvenient Dead*); and a collection of hope-filled stories of gender empowerment featuring a young Zapatista girl (*Once Upon a Time*).

Inspection of the Subcomandante's writings spanning some quarter-of-a-century reveal his extensive acquaintance with Mexican, Latin American, and Hispanic classics, and even World literature. Indeed, we find reference to a vast host of literary authors, including (but not limited to): Mario Benedetti, John Berger, Ray Bradbury, Berthold Brecht, Hector Aguilar Camín, Lewis Carroll, Miguel de Cervantes, G.K. Chesterton, Julio Cortázar, Roque Dalton, Dante Alighieri, Daniel Defoe, Eliseo Diego, Arthur Conan Doyle, Umberto Eco, Paul Éluard, Leon Felipe, Carlos Fuentes, Dario Fo, Adolfo Gilly, Ermilo Abreu Gómez, Miguel Hernández, Eric Jauffret, C.S. Lewis, Mario Vargas Llosa, Federico García Lorca, Antonio Machado, Hermann Melville, Manuel Vázquez Montalbán, Pablo Neruda, Cesare Pavese, Fernando Pessoa, Edmond Rostand, Juan Rulfo, Ernesto Sabato, Pedro Salinas, José Saramago, Manuel Scorza, William Shakespeare, Jonathan Swift, and Walt Whitman.

As for literary works and authors that Marcos has explicitly stated his fondness for, these include Juan Rulfo, James Joyce's *Ulysses*, the *Sonnets* of Shakespeare, *Don Quixote*, and anthologies of Miguel Hernández and Pablo Neruda, especially the latter's *Canto general*.[48] Regarding more contemporary writers, the Subcomandante has expressed his admiration for the Uruguayan authors Mario Benedetti and Eduardo Galeano.[49] Those who have conducted literary analyses of Marcos' writings have also pointed to the influence of Spanish literature, especially Cervantes' *Don Quixote*,[50] as well as the poetry of León Felipe, Miguel Hernández, and Frederico García Lorca.[51] Indeed, several observers have commented on the Subcomandante's familiarity with poetry, noting both how his "use of quotations, especially from poetry, seemed natural and effortless," and that "he is undoubtedly a good reader of Latin American poetry," with one going so far as to claim that Marcos himself "is in actual fact a poet."[52] Interestingly, when the Mexican Army seized the Subcomandante's H.Q., including his personal library, in its February 1995 offensive, they discovered books of poetry by Silvia Tomasa Rivera, Justo Sierra, Antón Makarenko, and Ernesto Zúñiga.[53]

The Subcomandante tells us that in addition to trying his hand at writing poetry as an adolescent, he also read, recited, and composed poems during his early years as a rural guerrilla in Chiapas, and that he also wrote "short narratives...much influenced by Cortázar..." adding "and in some of the stories... poetic elements appear...from Miguel Hernández, from Neruda from *Canto general.*"[54] Indeed, this period of relative seclusion in the mountains and canyons of Chiapas helped form Marcos as an author by shaping how he read and the way he engaged with his reading. Being able to carry around only a handful of books, among them "Pablo Neruda's *Canto general*...a selection of poems by Miguel Hernández, also poems by León Felipe, Cortázar's *Historias de cronopios y [de] famas*, the *Memoirs* of Francisco Villa, *Don Quixote*..."[55] Marcos tells us that "A book in those circumstances is something that...you read and re-read... and 'chew it over'...and finally many books were extracted from the one."[56]

Another significant influence on the Subcomandante's literary, and especially poetic, formation also took place at this time and was stimulated by his making contact, and interacting, with indigenous communities. Marcos told the Argentine poet Juan Gelman (1996) that:

> The way they [i.e. the indigenous] use language, the description of reality, of their world, has many poetical elements. That is how the normal or traditional cultural path I brought was altered, and that mixture began being produced which appeared in the EZLN communiqués of 1994.

The final stage in the Subcomandante's literary development came in the period following the 1994 uprising, during which, Marcos tells us, he "…went through that process of digestion throughout all those years of contact with…the people from outside, with civil society."[57] After a decade of social isolation the Subcomandante suddenly came into contact with the outside world, and most pertinently the prevailing intellectual and cultural currents that were then circulating. A number of eminent public intellectuals, both national and international, as well as prominent authors and cultural figures, began to interact with Marcos. Thus, John Berger, Carlos Fuentes, Eduardo Galeano, Adolfo Gilly, Eric Jauffret, and Luis Villoro exchanged letters with the Subcomandante. Others, including Argentine poet Juan Gelman, Colombian Nobel laureate Gabriel García Márquez, Spanish poet and detective novelist Manuel Vázquez Montalbán, and leading Mexican authors Carlos Monsiváis, Elena Poniatowska, and Guadalupe Loaeza, have sat down to talk with Marcos face-to-face. Such interactions undoubtedly stimulated Marcos intellectually and artistically, although he also claims that,

> I read more indigenous literature, poetry, legends.… And I am also nourished by oral exchange, when we talk with [the indigenous] Purépechas, Huicholes, Rarámuris, that helps us more for writing than just books. But a fundamental classic is *The Broken Spears: The Aztec Account of the Conquest of Mexico* [composed in part from translations of indigenous peoples' accounts of the Conquest] by Miguel León Portilla, that book was added to the nightstand.[58]

The Subcomandante's literary upbringing, which involved extensive and profound exposure to poetry and universal literature from early childhood; his own experimenting with composing verse at various stages of his life; his nourishment from prolonged, sustained and intimate contact with indigenous literature and peoples; and his interaction with national and international intellectual, literary, and cultural luminaries; all combined to influence greatly Marcos' approach toward, relationship with, and use of, language.

The Subcomandante himself provides us with a revealing insight into the origins of a tendency that is perhaps unique in the annals of Latin American left-wing guerrillas: namely, the privileging of literary references points, forms, and language over political ones in his political-philosophical discourse:

> My parents introduced us to García Márquez, Carlos Fuentes, Monsiváis, Vargas Llosa (regardless of his ideas), to mention only a few...I think this marked us. We didn't look out at the world through a news-wire but through a novel, an essay or a poem.... That was the prism through which my parents wanted me to view the world, as others might choose the prism of the media.... Strictly speaking we were already, as the orthodox [Left] would say, very corrupted by the time we got to...revolutionary literature. So that when we got into Marx and Engels we were thoroughly spoilt by literature; its irony and humour.[59]

Marcos' exposure to Marxism then, was both preceded and in turn shaped by literature, so that when he subsequently engaged with Marxist texts these were experienced and mediated through the pre-existing prism provided by his literary formation. This formation profoundly influenced the Subcomandante's discourse, shaping its points of reference, the forms that it took and the language it employed.

Taking these three elements in order: first, while Marcos' writings are peppered with references to literary authors, their works, and major characters, interestingly, the names of writers of political philosophy and their works are strikingly scarce.[60] Significantly, Kathleen Bruhn, after a comprehensive examination of the first three years of Zapatista communiqués (1994–1997), concluded that "Sherlock Holmes's sidekick, Dr. Watson, appears more often than Mexican union leader Fidel Velázquez, communist icon Vladimir Lenin, or Mexico's only indigenous president, Benito Juárez."[61] A concrete instance of the Subcomandante employing a literary reference, as opposed to a political one, to convey or reinforce his message can be seen when he discusses neoliberalism, which he dubs "The Catastrophic Political Management of Catastrophe." Here Marcos does not cite a Marxist text to explain his assertion that "The foundation of neoliberalism is a contradiction: in order to maintain itself it must devour itself and, therefore, destroy itself.… What keeps the system going is what will bring it down," but instead directs his readers to G.K. Chesterton's *The Three Horsemen of the Apocalypse*.[62]

Secondly, there is Marcos' choice of more literary (as opposed to strictly political) forms as the vehicles by which to carry his political messages. In his communiqués we encounter a variety of forms, including: fables, children's stories, first-hand reportage, literary vignettes, satirical monologues, dialogues between Marcos and his fictional alter egos, entertaining anecdotes relating everyday life in the guerrilla barracks or Zapatista communities, as well as indigenous myths, legends, and folktales. (Strikingly, Marcos even blends elements from diverse and sometimes contrasting genres within a single communiqué.) Many of these take the form of parables that promote plurality, tolerance, respect for difference, multiculturalism, and social inclusion, and that challenge entrenched racist, sexist, or anti-LGBTQ attitudes. The decision to employ literary genres no doubt stems from the Subcomandante's belief "that, often, the best texts of political analysis are [to be found] in universal literature…"[63] which finds expression in his assertion that:

> *Don Quixote* is the best book of political theory, followed by *Hamlet* and *Macbeth*. There is no better

way to understand the Mexican political system, in its tragic and comic aspects: *Hamlet, Macbeth* and *Don Quixote*.[64]

This conviction may have influenced Marcos' decision to co-author, alongside Paco Ignacio Taibo II, *The Uncomfortable Dead* or *The Inconvenient Dead* (*Muertos incómodos* in Spanish),[65] a detective novel that incorporates magical realism while articulating a pro-ecology, pro-democracy, anti-discriminatory (racial, gender, and sexual orientation), anti-neoliberal globalization, and anti-capitalist ethos.

Some have placed a good deal of importance on the poetic nature of Marcos' discourse. Elena Poniatowska, Mexico's "grande dame of letters" and arguably the country's most distinguished living writer, notes that "Marcos' words would not have had the same effect had…his political discourse not been also a poetic discourse" and has also stated that "His language is new in Mexican politics; it is the beginning of a new way of doing politics."[66] So too, Laura Hernández Martínez states that "…the most outstanding characteristic of Marcos' discourse is its poetic quality," which "appears much closer to the poetical than the political, [b]ut not because it pertains to this literary genre," but rather because it "renounces certainty…not only in the discourse which it opposes but also in its own discourse."[67] Meanwhile, Jérôme Baschet extols the Subcomandante's "narrative and linguistic abilities and his skill at weaving fable and story, humour and theory, social imaginary and tales of the everyday life of the native rebel communities into the heart of a discourse which is as political as it is poetical."[68] Similarly, Nicholas P. Higgins urges that Marcos' "telling choice of poetry as a favoured form of expression should not be acknowledged simply on the grounds of literary merit, but instead, it should be recognized as a conscious and political statement concerned with just how, and by whom, the realm of experience can best be communicated."[69] Finally, John Holloway claims that this "poetry…is not just a question of pretty words or of Marcos's undoubted literary skills...they offer a different way of seeing the world, a vision that breaks with the dominant logic of there-is-no-alternative."[70]

Thirdly, the poetical nature of the Subcomandante's discourse is connected with the language that he employs: more specifically, it marks a break with the kind of political discourse that typically had preceded him. Thus, Daniela Di Piramo notes that "Marcos' most effective prose...is totally different to traditional political literature...presenting serious political issues in a colourful and appealing manner that avoids the staidness of formal political rhetoric," while Jérôme Baschet argues that "the first virtue of... [Marcos'] use of language is that it breaks with conventions of customary political discourse, thanks to its humour, its irony and the continued recourse it has to a mixture of genres," adding "It is a matter also of breaking, by a concrete use of language, the abstractness of political theory, and it is here that the power of narratives works wonders."[71] Certainly, Marcos' use of language is refreshingly different from the insipid, formulaic and equivocating language typically employed by the politicians and government bureaucrats the world over whom we are accustomed to suffer today. However, it also broke, as several commentators have stressed,[72] with traditional leftist political rhetoric, which tended to be staid and heavily burdened with impenetrable Marxist terminology, creating instead a new political language that was as innovative and creative as it was inspiring and engaging. For this reason Marcos is attributed with having succeeded in "renewing" or "revitalizing" the language of the Left.[73]

Most crucially, however, Marcos' language also stands in stark contrast to that employed by the Mexican government, against which he has waged a war of words for the last quarter-of-a-century. Indeed, historian Lorenzo Meyer points out:

> The language of the Mexican political class, especially of those in power, has been, almost since its beginning, a murky language which has

multiple meanings and which conceals more than it uncovers … [and] is basically an instrument of disinformation, of systematic lies raised to an art form, whose central objective is the defense of illegitimate interests.[74]

Meyer then contrasts this with Marcos' discourse, which is "direct and simple—but not simplistic—and ha[s] some poetic license," and his language, which "is simple, comprehensible and has a clear moral foundation…[and] is, therefore, the antithesis of the governmental language." The Subcomandante himself would later point to the shortcomings of the language spouted by the Mexican government as playing a key role in prompting the formulation of the Zapatistas' discourse:

Evidently this is tied to the decline of a political system which had so massaged words as to have prostituted them. Taking back those concepts of nation, homeland, liberty, democracy and justice, the EZLN connected with a tradition of struggle, with a cultural tradition, and it produced this language which was able to permeate very symbolic strata in the society. It reached top intellectuals and very simple people, including the illiterate, that is, those with little baggage. We say that zapatismo knocked on a door, the door of political language. It found it open; it found that through it one could go many places and it gained access through it.[75]

Marcos would wield this language to great effect against the Mexican government, countering the hostile propaganda which it spewed out in an attempt to discredit the Zapatista cause and diminish the Subcomandante's popularity. Indeed, Marcos has often emphasized how, for the Zapatistas, "our weapons are words,"[76] inspiration for which he may have drawn from the French Marxist philosopher Louis Althusser, whose works he had studied intently at university and who had urged in his "Philosophy as a Revolutionary Weapon":

> In...political, ideological and philosophical struggle, the words are also weapons, explosives or tranquillizers and poisons. Occasionally, the whole class struggle may be summed up in the struggle for one word against another word. Certain words... are the site of an ambiguity: the stake in a decisive but undecided battle.... The philosophical fight over words is a part of the political fight.[77]

The Subcomandante's highly adept deployment of his arsenal of words led Mexican novelist and essayist, Jorge Volpi, when trying to account for "the fascination that Marcos provokes," to conclude that: "[T]he Subcomandante's unbridled prose, full of lyrical, humorous and sentimental effusions, is not simple boasting in order to confuse the enemy, but rather a careful strategy of combat[;]...his fight against injustice and discrimination and in favour of indigenous rights is based in large measure on his rhetorical skills."[78]

Finally, Marcos' practice of incorporating literary and poetic forms, styles, and influences that derived from both world literature and also indigenous literature (as well as local indigenous linguistic practices),[79] yielded considerable dividends in terms of maximizing the appeal of the Zapatistas' message globally. In a post-communist (or at least post-Soviet Union) world, it is highly doubtful that the Subcomandante would have been able to communicate successfully the movement's experience and message to the wider world, let alone garner broad (even global) public support for it, had he adopted the medium of an intensely technical Marxist discourse. In this way, he perhaps resembles George Orwell, who similarly chose to articulate his anti-imperialist, anti-totalitarian, left-wing messages not through overtly political treatises laden with leftist terminology but through novels, short stories, essays, and, most successfully, his masterpiece, the satirical and allegorical *Animal Farm*, which, it should be remembered, originally bore the subtitle "A Fairy Story." In other respects, Marcos conforms to the well-established tradition of political pamphleteers,[80] assailing Mexico's political elite with satirical barbs, lampooning their utterances and parodying their personalities, but with a postmodern twist on account of his choosing the medium of the Internet and his drawing on, and replicating, a plurality of genres.

CHAPTER 3

ANOTHER MEXICO

On the day they rose up, the Zapatistas distributed their own newspaper, titled *The Mexican Awakener*, in which was featured their "Declaration of War" and "Revolutionary Laws," as well as an "Editorial" (almost certainly penned by Marcos). In the latter, the ultimate aim of the movement was stated as being that of "building a new Mexico," and in the months that followed, the Subcomandante would again make reference both to "building" and "birthing" a "new Mexico."[81] In later years, he would modify his terminology slightly and talk of "fighting for another Mexico" and "building another Mexico."[82] As a means of engendering "another Mexico" (and ultimately "another world"), Marcos advocated and articulated "another way of doing politics," which he sometimes simply dubbed "another politics."

His first mention of this appears in a July 1996 communiqué in which he sets out "The Political Proposal of Zapatismo," stating "...our political position is [that] ... [w]e are against the state-party system, against presidentialism, and for democracy, liberty and justice, we are of the left, we are inclusive, and anti-neoliberal...this position...seeks to construct 'another' politics..."[83] The same month saw the Subcomandante giving a speech at the International Encuentro Against Neoliberalism and For Humanity in which he talked of the possibility of "produc[ing] another form of doing politics and another type of politician, other human beings that would do politics in a different way, unlike those people that we have to put up with today all across the political spectrum."[84]

In the years that followed, the Subcomandante made further (and more detailed) references to "another politics."[85] This was especially noticeable during the run-up to the 2006 presidential election, with the release of *The Sixth Declaration of the Lacandon Jungle* (2005), which contained several mentions of "another politics,"[86] and with the launching of The Other Campaign (2006), which bore the full title of The National Campaign with Another Politics for a National Program of Left-wing Struggle and for a New Constitution. Crucially, Marcos' call for "another politics" was no mere act of political sloganeering; rather, one of his chief contributions lies in his having helped very concretely to bring about "another way of doing politics" in respect to both indigenous politics in Mexico and national politics.

Taking these in order, the Subcomandante's impact on indigenous politics can be seen at both the local and national level. In Chiapas, both within the Zapatista army's own ranks and in the indigenous communities that acted as its support base, gender equality was actively promoted. This was something that was introduced and propagated by the urban, middle-class, university-educated, non-indigenous high-ranking members of the EZLN, such as Commander Elisa initially, and Subcomandantes Marcos, Pedro, and Daniel subsequently. The FLN, the mother organization of the EZLN, had drawn on and modelled itself according to a well-established tradition among Latin American revolutionary movements—including Cuba's revolutionaries, and more recently Nicaragua's Sandinistas and El Salvador's guerrillas—that broke with the continent's entrenched *machismo* by giving women prominence within their ranks. This tradition continued on with the EZLN in Chiapas and, after almost a decade of clandestine recruitment during which women belonging to the guerrilla organization enjoyed enhanced freedom and were promoted to positions of responsibility, it resulted in the drafting of the "Revolutionary Women's Law."

This law, which was initially applied solely to the EZLN's cadres and community support-base members, was extended throughout rebel-held territory following the Zapatistas' seizure of substantial tracts of land during and following the uprising. It mandated, among other things, that women had the right to education, as well as to:

> work and receive a fair salary; decide the number of children they will bear; participate in the affairs of the community and to hold positions of authority if they are freely and democratically elected; choose their partner and…not be forced into marriage; [and] occupy positions of leadership in the organization and to hold military ranks in the revolutionary armed forces.

The Law also stipulated harsh punishment for the physical mistreatment of women (such as beatings, rape, and attempted rape).[87] Moreover, even though the Subcomandante has continued to lament the limited progress being made within the Zapatista movement in relation to female political participation, as well as the persistence of disrespectful attitudes toward women and the rather uncooperative attitude of men toward sexual hygiene and contraception,[88] there can be absolutely no doubt that the deplorable plight of indigenous women improved considerably thanks to the endeavours of Marcos and other high-ranking EZLN officers, both male and female. In short, as a consequence of these efforts, the promotion and pursuit of women's rights became paramount not only among the Zapatista rank-and-file but also throughout the indigenous communities that sustained the movement.

Another change in indigenous politics that was brought about by Marcos in conjunction with other high-ranking Zapatistas was more restorative and modificatory than strictly innovative. This concerned the revival and revising of indigenous communal decision-making practices that functioned by means of consensus, the most notable of which being the holding of community assemblies. These practices, which were especially well-established among Tojolabal communities but which had fallen out of use or were in various states of abeyance in other indigenous communities, the EZLN leadership now revived and actively promoted, extending them throughout Zapatista territory and deepening the democratic process to be inclusive of women and to encourage female participation in what had previously been either exclusively male, or at least male-dominated, assemblies.

Turning to the issuing-in of "another" national politics, the Subcomandante helped transform the nation's political life by contributing to bringing about a more democratic and inclusive Mexico. This he did by: (1) facilitating the dissolution of the state-party system, (2) articulating a conception of democracy that far exceeded merely voting in national elections every six years, and (3) urging recognition of, and rights and respect for, ethnic and gender minorities. Of course, Marcos represented only the latest in a long line of those who had contributed to this lengthy and complex process of political transformation, although he proved arguably one of the most impassioned, eloquent and high-profile contributors.

Taking these in order, prior to 2000 Mexico had been governed by a single party, the Party of Institutional Revolution (PRI in Spanish), which had monopolized government for more than 70 years. This state-party system, as Marcos calls it, was one in which the PRI and the state had become so inextricably intertwined as to appear indistinguishable, with the result that corruption and electoral fraud were rife. The PRI government had been able to maintain itself in power so long largely by basing its legitimacy on certain key cornerstones. Put briefly, it portrayed itself as: the sole and rightful heir to, and continued upholder of the values of, the Mexican Revolution; both a bearer of modernity and a bestower of prosperity, through its neoliberal policies; and a guarantor of the Rule of Law. Marcos shattered this official portrait of the government by undermining the cornerstones upon which its legitimacy rested.

Undoubtedly, chief of these was the government's long-held, monopolistic grip on being the authentic, and therefore legitimate, exclusive heir to the Mexican Revolution. This the Subcomandante succeeded in wresting from the government through his re-appropriation of the figure of Zapata in the service of the Zapatista movement. As Marcos explained:

> When the EZLN...appeared, it had to fight the Mexican State for certain symbols of the nation's history. The terrain of symbols is an occupied terrain, above all as regards Mexican history...In this case, that of historic symbols, the Mexican State uses them in a way which must be fought over. Zapata, for example.[89]

So successful was the Subcomandante in this regard that the government withdrew Zapata's image from the ten peso note and President Salinas changed the backdrop of his televised statements from a hanging portrait of Zapata to one of Carranza. As a result, George A. Collier and Elizabeth L. Quaratiello point out: "These days, no one thinks of Zapata without thinking of Chiapas and Mexico's new indigenous movement...the ruling party has lost virtually any credible claim to Emiliano Zapata as one of its heroes."[90]

The second cornerstone propping up the government's legitimacy was its claim to have brought about Mexico's entry into modernity; indeed, this had been a substantial pillar of *salinismo*, President Salinas' (1988–1994) neoliberal economic orientation of the country. In an interview dated June 8, 1995, Carlos Monsiváis looked back over the preceding years, stating: "It was an incredible time. Rational, intelligent people were really in love with Salinas's ideas and Salinas's attitude...Salinas was the image of modernity...it was utter rubbish!"[91] In a later interview

Monsiváis recalled how "Before the rebellion in Chiapas, the key word in Mexico was 'modernization,' the illusion of the First World around the corner...'Modernization' took the place of nationalism, the old-time 'act' that united all sectors through festivity, mythology."[92]

Marcos immediately set about puncturing this myth of modernity; that is, the myth of Mexico as a democratic, first-world nation enjoying boons bestowed upon it by neoliberalism: interviewed on the first day of the uprising, the Subcomandante declared that "...the indigenous ethnicities of Mexico...are perfectly dispensable in the modernization program of Salinas de Gortari."[93] Subsequently, he would recall how, through their uprising "thousands of indigenous armed with truth and fire, with shame and dignity, shook the country awake from its sweet dream of modernity," and talked of "the crime that, disguised as modernity, distributes misery on a global scale."[94] He would also boast sarcastically in a 1995 communiqué that:

> History written by Power taught us that we had lost, that cynicism and profit were virtues, that honesty and sacrifice were stupid, that individualism was the new god, and hope was devalued money, without currency in the international markets, without purchasing power...We did not learn the lesson. We were bad pupils. We did not believe what Power taught us. We skipped school when in class they taught conformism and idiocy. We failed [the subject of] modernity.[95]

Similarly, in a November 2013 communiqué, the Subcomandante railed against those who come to Zapatista communities extolling the virtues of modernity and so-called progress: "They tell us all this while clumsily editing out the fact that it is in their modernity where the most atrocious crimes are committed...

where inhumanity is rewarded and exalted and any ethical or moral value is a symptom of 'cultural backwardness.'"[96]

However, the Subcomandante's most eloquent statement on the subject, and the one which perhaps has elicited the most resonance, came in a communiqué dated January 20, 1994:

> by taking off its own mask, Mexican civil society will realize, with a stronger impact, that the image that it has sold itself is forgery, and that reality is far more terrifying than it thought. Each of us will show our faces, but the big difference will be that "Sup Marcos" has always known what his real face looked like, and civil society will just wake up from a long and tired sleep that "modernity" has imposed at the cost of everything and everyone.[97]

The result, as George A. Collier and Elizabeth L. Quaratiello observe, was as follows:

> At the time of the Zapatista rebellion, Mexico was synonymous with "economic modernization".... At least for a time, the Zapatistas successfully deflected attention away from those who were pursuing modernization at any cost, and they forced a change in the public discourse over Mexico's future.... During 1994, the Zapatista rebellion seemed to stop the steamroller of Salinas de Gortari's modernizing project in its tracks.[98]

A crucial and integral aspect of Salinas' modernization project was neoliberal economic reform. As Marcos outlined in one interview,

> Salinas de Gortari's strategy within neoliberalism was to construct a publicity campaign, presenting abroad a stable country, a good product that he was

> selling.... [W]e managed to affect that publicity campaign...to...demonstrate what was really happening, what this political, economic project meant for this country, for a part of the country, for the indigenous.

He continued:

> Society is beginning to march in one direction and the State, the political system, in another...one is talking about two Mexicos: the virtual one of the political class with its great economic successes, the 7.5% Gross National Product growth and that of the rest of society which does not see economic growth anywhere.[99]

After the financial debacle of late 1995, the Subcomandante would proclaim that "Neoliberalism is not a theory to confront or explain the crisis. It is the crisis itself made theory and economic doctrine!"[100] He also repeatedly decried the evils of neoliberalism in a series of tales involving imaginary "conversations" between the Subcomandante and one of his most famous literary creations, the beetle Don Durito of the Lacandon Jungle.[101]

The final cornerstone of the government's legitimacy that was undermined by the Subcomandante was the Rule of Law, which the government frequently claimed to be upholding in an unconvincing attempt to maintain legitimacy. Indeed, this is a theme that Marcos returned to several times in his communiqués. For example, in a June 1995 communiqué he writes: "No longer able to win legitimacy, incapable of struggling to achieve it, Power dresses itself with 'legality.' The legal mantle can do anything... including the violation of the law. That is how the mirror of Power works, with a legal although illegitimate image."[102] So too, in a September 1995 communiqué the Subcomandante— describing both the government's February offensive which contravened the ceasefire it had agreed with the EZLN, and the mass demonstrations that this action provoked on the part of civil society—wrote: "Trying to cover the lack of legitimacy of their actions with the thin veil of legality the evil government put the entire country at the edge of a civil war.... The so-called 'Iruegas' doctrine, the strategy that replaces legitimacy with legality, failed."[103]

Marcos also exposed how the government had donned a "Rule-of-Law mask" in order to disguise its practice of persecuting the poor while protecting the rich:

> Lacking the legitimacy which can only be obtained by the governed, these characters from the Mexican tragedy at the end of the century, supplant it with a mask made "ex profeso," that of the Rule of Law. In the name of the "Rule of Law" they impose economic measures, they assassinate, they imprison, they rape, they destroy, they persecute, they make war.... On top of this...nightmare cocktail, in addition to their poverty, millions of Mexicans will now have to take responsibility for the rescue of those other criminals, the bankers, who use the "Rule of Law" as an alibi, and who have an ever-willing accomplice and procurer in the Government. [104]

In a speech at the inauguration of a Zapatista-convened forum on the reform of the state (July 1, 1996), Marcos went even further, stating "That which kills a person is homicidal. That which kills many [people] is genocidal. What should one call that which kills a nation? The Mexican political system calls it 'the rule of law.'"[105]

The Subcomandante's highly effective undermining of these cornerstones upon which the State-party's legitimacy rested meant that, as Andrej Grubačić and Deni O'Hearn point out, "The historic defeat of the PRI was widely regarded as a consequence of the Zapatista movement," with them adding that, "As an 'external challenge' to the PRI, and to the national political system as a whole, the Zapatistas accelerated Mexico's democratization."[106]

Marcos' contribution to democratizing Mexico was not, however, limited to helping dismantle the state-party. Rather, it involved a constructive component too, namely, proposing a different concept of democracy to that which was commonly envisioned. We catch a glimpse of this in numerous Zapatista communiqués penned by the Subcomandante that address democracy. In one, for example, he emphasizes how "For the Zapatistas, democracy is much more than the electoral contest or alternation in power.... [We] struggle for democracy, not *only* for electoral democracy, but *also* for electoral democracy."[107] However, Marcos' clearest articulations on this topic can be found in certain interviews he has given. He told esteemed French sociologist and Latin American specialist, Yvon Le Bot, that "The concept of democracy should include many aspects of the democratic life of the country," noting how "it must be recognized that other types of non-representative democracies exist...other kinds of democracy which are practiced in unions, student organizations, in neighbourhoods, in rural communities...communitarian democracy or direct democracy or social democracy."[108] In a subsequent interview Marcos further elaborated on what form he envisions this democracy taking:

> We fight for a democracy that will create a new relationship between those who govern and those who are governed, what we have called 'command-obeying'.... In the new relationship that we are proposing, representative democracy would be more balanced. It would enrich itself with direct democracy, with the continual participation of the citizens, not only as electors or as consumers of electoral proposals, but also as political actors.... We are trying to encourage the increased participation

of citizens. We want them to be more watchful that those who govern are fulfilling society's needs, that they take decisions and issue mandates, under the command of the citizens, mindful of those who they govern.... We believe that there should be a system of permanent evaluation of a government's work. We propose a mechanism of sanction, which will function not only as punishment but also in the form of positive recognition. When an elected party is not fulfilling its role, these mechanisms should also permit society to reverse a decision that has been made during an electoral process.[109]

Crucially, in the same interview, the Subcomandante also makes the connection between democracy and social inclusion, and stresses the need for the latter:

The other fundamental aspect of the democracy that we want for Mexico is the recognition of differences and rights. Because there is no average or ordinary Mexican, and each social group has its differences, the democracy that we want must recognize these rights and not impose the rights of some above the rest. It is most obvious in the case of the indigenous, but equally you could talk about groups like homosexuals, lesbians, the disabled, the retired, all those who have specific differences and therefore should have specific rights.[110]

Regarding indigenous peoples specifically, one of the Subcomandante's chief accomplishments in promoting ethnic inclusivity came from his challenging of the PRI-State's racial ideology, *mestizaje*, which exalted the blending of indigenous and non-indigenous races and/or cultures, and which the state-party drew on in order to foster national unity and promote social cohesion. Although seemingly benign, this ideology, while it lauded Mexico's indigenous past, entailed the disparagement of contemporary indigenous peoples, as José Rabasa explains:

> The state-sponsored ideology of *mestizaje* after the 1910 Revolution theoretically should have extended bonds of solidarity with Indians, but its historical effect was to promote a systematic denial of Indian roots—though the pre-Columbian past was idealized—and a program of acculturation that aimed to destroy indigenous languages and cultures. Only "mestizos" were deemed by the state to be authentic Mexicans.[111]

Marcos basically exploded the myth of *mestizaje*, and challenged the Mexican government's premise that indigenous peoples had to abandon their ethnic and cultural identities and assimilate culturally into a hegemonic *mestizo* nation state in order to be both fully accepted as Mexican citizens and included in mainstream Mexican society. He also laid bare to *mestizo* Mexico, through his eloquence and satirical wit, *mestizaje*'s inherently racist nature and discriminatory function. In doing so, he provoked much soul searching throughout *mestizo* society, especially among Mexico's public intellectuals. For example, Nobel laureate Octavio Paz claimed that "we are all responsible because we have permitted, in Chiapas and in other regions of Mexico, the perpetuation of the misery of the peasants and, especially, of the indigenous communities,"[112] while Carlos Monsiváis noted that with the Zapatista uprising "Mexican racism has been exposed for the first time at a national level," adding "for the first time in Mexican history we have begun to problematize racism, the misery and inequality with respect to Indian rights."[113]

In particular, the Subcomandante savaged the government for its hypocritical, callous, and calculating policy toward the indigenous, whereby it utilized Mexico's Indian past as a tourist attraction while condemning present-day indigenous peoples to live in a state of abject neglect. As Marcos explained to one interviewer,

> The government...want[s] to show the tourists the lovely Mexican culture...the folkloric dancing, the beautiful clothing and crafts of the indigenous people. But behind this picture is the real Mexico, the Mexico of the millions of Indians who live in extreme poverty. We have helped peel off the mask to reveal the real Mexico.[114]

The Subcomandante's efforts to promote inclusivity toward Mexico's indigenous peoples were not limited to targeting the government and its policies however. Instead, he strove to erode entrenched attitudes of racism that persisted, and were prevalent, in Mexican society as a whole. This he did not only through the political statements, declarations and arguments that he made in his communiqués but also by means of the stories he often appended to these. Indeed, Marcos has penned numerous tales featuring as the protagonist Old Antonio, a Mayan elder who introduces the Subcomandante, and thus ultimately Marcos' *mestizo* readership, to the folklore, values, worldview and way of life of Chiapas' indigenous peoples. More than this however, by having the literary character of "Marcos" act as a foil to Old Antonio in these stories, the Subcomandante challenged *mestizo* preconceptions and stereotypes regarding indigenous peoples, and subverted a lingering ethnic hierarchy based on prejudiced perceptions of cultural superiority. As Cornelia Graebner observes:

> The[se] stories featuring the Mayan elder Old Antonio and the conceited *guerrillero* "Marcos" express the personal and cultural element of the encounter between the indigenous and the *mestizo*, and of the shared political struggle that emerges from

this encounter.... The friendship between the two characters stages the possibility of dialogue between worlds that are radically "other" to each other.[115]

Arguably Marcos' most significant contribution toward making Mexico more inclusive of its indigenous peoples however can be seen in his championing of indigenous rights and culture, especially in connection with their demands for autonomy (i.e. the right to organize and govern themselves economically, politically, and culturally according to indigenous customs and practices). True, neither he, nor even the Zapatista movement as a whole, were the first to propose or even promote indigenous autonomy. However, as anthropologist Héctor Díaz-Polanco has pointed out, "with the Zapatista uprising the theme of autonomy acquired a national relevance, democratic vigour and a more defined profile"; with another expert in this field, Shannan L. Mattiace, stating that "the EZLN uprising provided a space for Indian and non-Indian activists and intellectuals to discuss and debate the issue of Indian Rights and culture in Mexico," adding "...indigenous peoples have greatly expanded the use and meaning of 'autonomy' since the Zapatista uprising."[116]

Naturally, the Subcomandante's high profile, eloquence, charisma, and position of authority based on having lived alongside indigenous peoples on a day-to-day basis for over a decade prior to the 1994 uprising, combined to make him an extremely effective advocate for and publicist of indigenous rights and autonomy. He succeeded, for example, in squarely placing indigenous rights on the national political agenda, and contributed significantly to putting substantial pressure on the government to legally recognize autonomy by amplifying indigenous peoples' calls for such recognition. The Subcomandante also conveyed indigenous people's desire for autonomy and the justice of their demand for it so effectively that the idea gained broad traction among, and wide acceptance with, audiences in Mexico and abroad. At the same time that Marcos was garnering support and engendering solidarity for indigenous autonomy, he managed to disarm the specious arguments of the government and right-wing nationalists who sought to turn public opinion against the idea by misrepresenting it as a call for separatism or secession.

Finally, and crucially, Marcos also tapped into—and stimulated further—a growing sense of pride among Mexico's various indigenous peoples in their ethnic identity, contributing to the consolidation, amplification and broadening of an emerging spirit of solidarity, a common feeling of being fellow indigenous peoples who were experiencing the same problems and confronting the same obstacles to their shared hopes and dreams. This he was able to do by using his high public profile as spokesperson for the indigenous Zapatista movement, and perhaps most notably by both helping to forge a close relationship with Mexico's National Indigenous Congress and heading the 2001 and 2006 Zapatista tours of the country during which the Subcomandante reached out to indigenous peoples as he passed through their communities stopping to give speeches and meeting face-to-face to talk with them. Ultimately then, Marcos aided indigenous peoples in extending the scope of their aspirations beyond their immediate locales to the regional and even national level.

In addition to urging both the rejection of discrimination against, and a genuine respect for, ethnic minorities, Marcos also championed the rights of gendered minorities, meaning both women[117] and members of the lesbian, gay, bisexual, and transgender (LGBTQ) community. Significantly, as early as May 28, 1994, in a communiqué that Marcos wrote in response to the media and public's fascination with discovering his true identity, and in which he declared "Marcos is…every untolerated, oppressed, exploited minority that is resisting and saying, 'Enough!',", the Subcomandante drew attention to the discrimination faced by, among many others, gays and women in certain roles or situations. "Marcos is gay in San Francisco," he proclaimed, "a housewife in any neighborhood in any city in any part of Mexico on a Saturday night...a woman alone in a Metro station at 10 p.m."[118] Marcos would spend the next two decades devoting significant time and energy to highlighting the plight of women and LGBTQs, and to celebrating their resistance to the discrimination they frequently suffer.

In January 2009, for example, the Subcomandante would reflect on the support that the Zapatistas had received over the years from specifically women and LGBTQs (as well as indigenous peoples and young people), and attributed this solidarity to the fact that "we have in common the status of being 'others,' excluded, discriminated against, feared."[119] He then went on to talk of how society imposes a "norm or standard" whereby everything is classified, with anything not readily classifiable being "labelled with a sign: The Other." The Subcomandante continues:

> Of course, these classifications are also descriptions, and with them comes a series of cultural codes and behavioural guidelines that must be followed. A type of survival manual that human beings do not receive in a bound copy, but assimilate in doses— brutal doses most of the time—over the long or short course of their maturation—that is, their domestication. Think about it like a *What to Do When*...brochure.

> And like this, unwritten but evident and omnipresent, there would be brochures for... *What to Do When around Women* or... *What to Do When around Gays, Lesbians, Transgender People, or Transsexuals*.... The collection could be called *Be a Normal Person* and be released in collectible instalments...[and] these "education" or "survival in normalcy" manuals...have things in common:

"Distrust!" "Despise!" "Discriminate!" "Assault!" "Mock!" These would be a few.

And in their particularities we could find the following:

...*What to Do When around Women* would say: "If you are a man, look at her like what she is, like an object, like a whore with an owner or still without an owner. If you are a woman, do the same. Value her based on her potential for sexual use, her labor power, or as a decorative element. Assault her. If she's good, grope her, take her, make her yours, or at least try. If the use of force is necessary, don't hesitate, use it. Let that object you have know who's in charge and know that we are not all equal."

We must not be afraid to say it; this manual is extremely widespread and is practiced enthusiastically among the sector of men or males who say that we are below and to the left. Silencing it, hiding it, does not absolve us of guilt or exorcize the spectre: sometimes we look too much like what we claim to fight against....

And in the brochure on *What to Do When around Gays, Lesbians, Transgender People, or Transsexuals* one would read: "Assume that you are with a diseased criminal, so back away (we have not ruled out the possibility that whoredom may be contagious). If you have children, keep them at a distance. In extreme cases, go to your chief confessor (note: in their absence, a member of the PAN, or of any right-wing party, will do)."

Let's say it: not only with women, also with different sexual preferences, the Left is deeply sexist. And the Zapatistas? Maybe we are the same or worse. In the best-case scenario, we have a long way to go. But with a determination to learn and, above all, with the spaces that make that learning possible and with the teachers: you.

In the case of women, the Subcomandante of course contributed massively to improving the lot of indigenous women's lives in Zapatista communities, although he has acknowledged that there remains much to be done. However, he has also spoken out against treatment that women in general often experience, especially those living in macho, often chauvinistic, Mexico. For instance, in *The Sixth Declaration of the Lacandon Jungle* (2005) Marcos applauds the fact that in Mexico "there are women who won't let themselves be treated as ornaments or be humiliated and despised just for being women, who are organizing and fighting for the respect they deserve."[120]

So too, in May 2006 Marcos gave a presentation in Mexico City at the "Women without Fear" event that had been organized to protest the recent imprisonment, beating, sexual assault, and even rape of female demonstrators by police and security forces at Atenco.[121] In his speech before the predominantly female crowd the Subcomandante introduced himself as follows:

My name is Subcomandante Insurgente Marcos, and I am, among other things, the spokesperson for the EZLN…and among the numerous personal flaws I bear, sometimes cynically and cockily, is that of being a man, macho, male. As such I must bear, and often flaunt, a series of archetypes, clichés, proofs. Not only in regard to me and my sex, but also and above all in reference to woman, the female gender.

In the course of his presentation, not only did the Subcomandante condemn the violence perpetrated against the female protesters seized at Atenco, he also broadened the discussion to include condemnation of how women are generally treated in Mexico, and especially how they are forced "to travel through life begging pardon and asking permission for being, and in order to be, women."

In particular, Marcos seized on a recent, highly chauvinistic statement by former-president Vicente Fox in which the then-senator called women "two-legged washing machines," and spent much of the presentation developing the metaphor of women as "machines of pleasure and work…[which] include assembly instructions which the dominant system assigns them." The Subcomandante observes how:

> In the assembly instructions for the merchandise known as "Woman," it explains that the model should always have her head bowed. That her most productive position is on her knees. That the brain is optional, and its inclusion is often counterproductive. That her heart should be nourished with trivialities. That her spirit should be maintained by competition with others of her same gender in order to attract the buyer, that always unsatisfied customer, the male. That her ignorance should be fed in order to guarantee better functioning. That the product is capable of self-maintenance and improvement (and there is a wide range of products for that, in addition to salons…). That she should not only learn to reduce her vocabulary to "yes" and "no," but, above all, she should learn when she should speak these words…. Women should serve men, always following those instructions, in order to be absolved of the crime of being a woman.

The presentation culminates in Marcos extolling the courage of those women who resist this process:

> Women confront this assembly process twenty-four hours a day, 365 days a year, from the moment they are born until the day that they die—at home, in the fields, on the street, at school, in the workplace, on transportation, in culture, in art, entertainment, science, government. But there are women who confront it with rebellion. Women who, instead of asking permission, command their own existence. Women who, instead of begging pardon, demand justice.... [T]he assembly instructions say that women should be submissive and walk on their knees. And, nonetheless, some women are naughty and walk upright. There are women who tear up the assembly instructions and stand up on their feet. There are women without fear.

In addition to making such explicit declarations openly criticizing the sexism and misogyny that women commonly face in Mexico (and in the world), the Subcomandante also sought to undermine traditional macho values through more subtle means, namely by penning numerous stories that subvert chauvinistic stereotypes. Some of these apologues feature interactions among Zapatista children in which boys are bested by girls; in other stories male Zapatista troops are outdone in some way or another by their female counterparts; and in still more Marcos himself is outmatched by an array of Zapatista girls and female officers. Moreover, from 2015 we find the Subcomandante introducing a new character into his stories: a small indigenous girl aged around ten called "Zapatista Defence" (owing to the position she plays in a Zapatista soccer team that she is putting together) who attends a Zapatista autonomous school. She is portrayed as being feisty, fearless even, as having verbal diarrhea, and as swearing and cursing a lot, especially when raging against patriarchy. In "The Apocalypse According to *Defensa Zapatista*," for example, she ridicules the way men act "all macho," with "their songs about horses and love and then about lost love," and how "they want us women to just be waiting on them hand and foot, and then later they tell us how much they love us and how we have very pretty eyes."[122]

Marcos also relates anecdotes—whether they are true or made up is unknown and of only secondary importance—in which he again challenges both chauvinistic assumptions and stereotypes, as well as entrenched, prevailing sexist attitudes. We have, for example, Marcos' 2009 tale entitled "Marxism According to Insurgent Erika," in which a female insurgent attributes this particular political philosophy to one Karla Marx, and in which the following exchange takes place:

Marcos: I thought that he was a man and that his name was Karl Marx.

Erika: Ah, but that's a damn old husbands' tale, it came to my thoughts that she was a woman.[123]

We also have an anecdote in which Marcos relates how, after he had received a coy and evasive answer on the part of Erika as to which movie the Zapatista troops were about to watch, he sneaked into the viewing tent and found them watching a Jean-Claude Van Damme film:

I turned toward Insurgent Erika and asked: "And why couldn't you tell me that you were going to watch a movie about karate?"

"It wasn't exactly this movie, Marcos," Insurgent Erika responded and turned toward the other compañeras, as if asking for help.

The public health insurgent came to the rescue and she declared: "No compañero Subcomandante, the thing is that the movie we were going to watch is one about sexual health, about diseases and hygiene and those things."

"Yes, about AIDS," said Erika, now feeling supported by the other woman.... It turns out that the female insurgents wanted to watch the movie "about AIDS," to use Erika's words, and the men wanted to watch *Lionheart,* which, by the way, they had already seen like 365 times. They couldn't agree and they argued and, as it should not be, the women won and they watched the movie "about AIDS." The men, too, because the women promised that if they watched the movie "about AIDS," they would watch Van Damme afterward. And they kept their word.

To provide a final anecdote (though many others exist), the Subcomandante reports his dressing down by a more senior female commander:

Several days ago we met to talk about how the Sandinista commander Mónica Baltodano was going to come. One of the female commanders brought up that phrase that the Sandinista women used to say that goes: "Revolution cannot be made without the participation of women." I jokingly told her that I was going to make a phrase that went: "Revolution can be made in spite of women." The commander looked down at me from above, just like it says in the manual, and told me: "Err, Marcos, we are waging a war for liberation. If it's taking us a while, it's because of the goddamn men."

More recently, at the Zapatista seminar titled Critical Thought in the Face of the Capitalist Hydra held in May 2015, the Subcomandante incorporated into one of his presentations the words of several non-indigenous Zapatista women on the sexism they frequently encounter and what they see as the way forward regarding feminism, using the occasion to give voice to this rarely heard constituency. Specifically, he repeats these women's condemnations of: the misguided but entrenched belief among some men that women dress purely to please them; the macho stupidity of those men who think women are "prize game" to "hunt"; being cat-called in the street; the sexual harassment they encounter both at work and on public transport; the attempts by men to get them into bed by pretending to be interested in the Zapatista struggle; and the verbal abuse they receive if they reject a man's advances; as well as expressing a host of other grievances. He also conveys these women's key messages: namely, that the women of Zapatista communities are exemplary since "with their struggle, their history, they show us that each must make their own way"; that ultimately "there are as many feminisms as there are women, because each of us has our own way, each of us has our own history, our own ghosts, our own fears, and each of us is figuring out how to fight them and defeat them"; and that "Zapatismo…makes you want to be a better person, a better woman." Through the Subcomandante's decision to publicize them, the views and experiences of these women were able to reach a national and international audience.[124]

Just as the Subcomandante helped shine a spotlight on the discrimination that women frequently face, so too he also focused attention on the struggle of the LGBTQ community. In June 1999 he sent a message of respect, solidarity, and support to the Committee of Sexual Diversity and to the lesbian, gay, bisexual, and transsexual community as a whole on the occasion of their "21st March of Lesbian, Gay, Bisexual, and Transsexual Pride." In it he wrote,

For a very long time, homosexuals, lesbians, transsexuals and bisexuals have had to...bear having their humanness reduced for the simple fact of not being in accord with a nonexistent sexual norm.... From all social sectors, from all corners of the country, from all workplaces, from studies, from struggles, from life: a human demand is raised: respect and recognition for the rights of the lesbian, gay, transsexual and bisexual community.[125]

In an interview with Gabriel García Marquéz in 2001 the Subcomandante again emphasized the marginality of sexual minorities, stating "Even if we Zapatistas all removed our balaclavas we would not be a minority in the same way that homosexuals, lesbians, transsexuals are."[126] And by 2002 scholar Cynthia Steele was already noting how Marcos "increasingly includes discussions of feminist and gay struggles in his chronicles."[127]

This focus on gender minorities, and especially LGBTQs, intensified in 2005 and 2006. First came the release of *The Sixth Declaration of the Lacandon Jungle*, which lauded for their resistance toward neoliberalism "...homosexuals, lesbians, transsexuals who won't put up with being ridiculed, despised, mistreated and even killed for having another way that is different, who do not accept being treated like they are abnormal or criminals, but who make their own organizations in order to defend their right to be different."[128] Then came the publication of the Subcomandante's and Paco Ignacio Taibo II's joint novel, *The Uncomfortable Dead* or *The Inconvenient Dead*, which features such characters as a homosexual Filipino mechanic named Juli@, a lesbian German motorbike pizza deliverer, and a transsexual called Magdalena who reappears as a protagonist in several subsequent stories by Marcos. Finally, there came The Other Campaign, which was launched by the Zapatistas in 2006 and saw Marcos at its head touring the nation. Very early on in the campaign, the Subcomandante reached out to members of the LGBTQ community, many of whom responded warmly to his overtures.

A notable specific instance from this campaign took place on the evening of February 9, in the main plaza of the town of Oaxaca, when the Subcomandante addressed an audience several thousand strong, accompanied on the bandstand by Leonardo Tlahui, a queer activist, artist, writer, and founding member of the Nancy Cardenas Sexual Diversity Collective in Oaxaca. Tlahui delivered a speech immediately before Marcos spoke in which he called for recognition of the contributions made by members of the queer community both to society in general but also to social struggles in particular, to which Marcos responded by declaring the Zapatistas' continued commitment to struggling against discrimination toward, and for respect regarding, members of the LGBTQ community. An observer of The Other Campaign noted at the time the importance of Marcos' gesture of inclusion toward LGBTQs:

> On his "Other Campaign"...Subcomandante Marcos regularly invites the participation of workers, farmers, indigenous peoples, women, youth and elders in constructing a national anti-capitalist campaign, "from below and to the left." But perhaps alone among nationally-recognized political leaders he adds gays and lesbians—what he frequently refers to as the community of "other loves"—to the list of people who fight for a new Mexico and who the Zapatistas seek to ally with in a larger struggle.... This has been significant not only because the historic sectors of revolutionary movements in Mexico (workers, students and campesinos) have excluded or ignored queer liberation politics, but also because beyond lip service, there hasn't been an opportunity previously to build connection and dialogue in such a way.[129]

This principle of social inclusion, which entails the utter rejection of the practice of excluding certain minorities, be they indigenous peoples, women or members of the LGBTQ community, is one that Marcos has consistently emphasized and which he clearly feels is integral to the Zapatista project. Indeed, when outlining the precise nature of the Zapatistas' political philosophy and practice, the Subcomandante wrote,

> *Zapatismo is not an ideology,*
> *it is not a bought and paid for doctrine.*
> *It is…an intuition.*
> *Something so open and flexible that it really occurs in all places.*
> *Zapatismo poses the question:*
> *"What is it that has excluded me?"*
> *"What is that has isolated me?"*
> *…In each place the response is different.*
> *Zapatismo simply states the question*
> *and stipulates that the response is plural,*
> *that the response is inclusive…* [130]

Given the Subcomandante's efforts to "destroy this…state system…[and] open up…a democratic space where the political parties, or groups that aren't parties, can air and discuss their social proposals…"[131]; his proposing of the enrichment of electoral or representative democracy with direct or participatory democracy (and particularly his advocacy of "command-obeying"); his urging of the creation of "a popular, autonomous legislative power, independent and critical [that] would be a resounding blow to the arbitrary authoritarianism of the presidential system in Mexico";[132] and his insistence on a political system that is inclusive of minorities; it is not surprising to find numerous commentators stressing Marcos' democratic credentials and praising his contribution to democratizing Mexico. Thus, Enrique Krauze asserts that "Marcos and his movement have been enormously helpful to Mexico in helping to accelerate political and democratic reform"; while Jorge Volpi declares that "the words of the *Subcomandante* produced demonstrable effects: without a doubt, his voice…contributed to the democratization of the country…"[133] The Subcomandante's (and his fellow Zapatistas') emphasis on democracy and inclusion in turn helps explain the movement's enormous and wide-ranging appeal. As Alex Khasnabish notes, "The radically democratic nature of Zapatismo is one of the key elements that drew others within and outside of Mexico to the Zapatista struggle following the rebellion."[134]

More than this, however, Marcos' entry into Mexico's national politics saw the advent of a political figure who commands respect based on the fact that he genuinely champions the indigenous, women, LGBTQs, as well as the poor and downtrodden, and does so from a position of moral authority, with many, among them eminent Mexican public intellectuals, seeing his life choices, and especially his living among the indigenous and sharing their daily hardships, as "admirable."[135] As renowned Mexican author Elena Poniatowska put it in 1995:

> In a country hungry for figures worthy of looking up to, the element of ethics in Marcos's identity is definitive. He has…raised our society's consciousness, he has made that society participatory. Thanks to him, and I don't blush to say it, I think we are better people. At least Marcos hasn't lied to us, he has not betrayed anybody, and he has lived according to his ideas, which seems to be a lot to ask in our country. He stayed in the jungle for eleven years, he has shared and continues to share the Indians' living conditions, he means what he says, and he keeps his word.[136]

For many then, the Subcomandante represents a principled and incorruptible political figure possessed of vision and passion (not to mention the eloquence to convey these in an appealing and effective manner), who has practiced considerable self-sacrifice and who offers hope to progressive and left-wing sectors of Mexican society. As such, he stands in stark contrast with Mexico's politicians—the most discredited profession in the nation according to Mexican-American essayist, cultural commentator and literature critic Ilan Stavans[137]—who are widely perceived as self-serving (i.e. as having entered politics not in a spirit of public service but out of self-enrichment and self-promotion) and as speaking "a murky language...of systematic lies raised to an art form."[138]

In these ways, Marcos contributed substantially to formulating and practising "another politics." Of course, it would be a gross misrepresentation to suggest that the Subcomandante was solely responsible for these changes to indigenous politics and national politics that have been taking place in Mexico over a period of decades. Indeed, countless others past and present have laboured, often unseen, toward the same ends, making their own unique contributions to making Mexico more democratic and inclusive. That being said, there can be no doubt that Marcos represented the latest, most high-profile, and arguably therefore most influential, in a procession of figures who have striven to effect such changes, and so must be attributed with having helped considerably in bringing about "another politics," and through this, ultimately, "another Mexico," a "new Mexico."

CHAPTER 4

ANOTHER WORLD

From before the end of the very first month of the uprising it was clear that while the Zapatistas' military actions were limited to the state of Chiapas, their vision was not. The Subcomandante in particular had set his sights on a far more distant horizon: during the first months of 1994 Marcos spoke of envisioning not only a "new Mexico" but also a "new world."[139] In a communiqué dated March 1, 1994, (i.e. exactly two months after the uprising began), he elaborated on this vision:

> In our dreams we have seen another world. A sincere world, a world definitively more just than the one in which we now move. We saw that in this world armies were not necessary; peace, justice, and freedom were so common in it that no one spoke of them as far-off things, but as one mentions bread, birds, air, water, as one says book and voice, that's how the good things in this world were spoken of. And in this world, the government of the majority was fair and followed the will of the people, and those who directed the people thought well; they directed while obeying.[140]

In October of the same year the Subcomandante would write a letter to former political prisoner, author, and professor Adolfo Gilly in which he revealed the scope of the Zapatistas' revolutionary proposal, stating that "the…thing we have proposed is changing the world." Almost a year later, Marcos ended a September 1995 communiqué that he sent to those attending a meeting in Brescia (Italy) convoked to express solidarity regarding the situation in Chiapas with the assertion that, "It is not necessary to conquer the world, it is sufficient to make it anew."[141] Less than a year later, in the summer of 1996, the Zapatistas would convene an Intercontinental Gathering, one which billed itself not as being concerned with the limited goal of achieving social justice for the indigenous of Chiapas but rather as being "For Humanity and Against Neoliberalism." The invitation to this event, which was penned by the Subcomandante, declared that,

> Zapatismo is not a new political ideology or a rehash of old ideologies…. There are no universal recipes, lines, strategies, tactics, laws, rules or slogans. There is only a desire: to build a better world, that is, a new world.[142]

Moreover, Marcos would continue to voice similar ambitions. For example, in a communiqué dated September 14, 1997, the Subcomandante vowed,

> We'll build another world.
> A better one.
> Bigger.
> Better.
> One in which all worlds can fit.[143]

Less than two years later, in a communiqué dated June 1999, he urged:

> It is possible to have another world, different than what the violent supermarket of neoliberalism is selling us. It is possible to have another world

> where the choice is between war and peace,
> between memory and forgetting, between hope and
> resignation, between grey tones and the rainbow. It
> is possible to have a world where many worlds fit.[144]

More recently, in 2008, having not long returned from The Other Campaign, during which the Subcomandante had toured the country listening to the humble and downtrodden individually tell of their personal experience of dispossession and exploitation, but also of their resistance to such treatment, Marcos and the Zapatistas convened The Global Festival of Dignified Rage with its theme of "Another World, Another Path: Below and to the Left." In his communiqué announcing the forthcoming Festival, Marcos urged: "Let us listen to each other then, let us know each other. Let our rage grow and become hope.... If this world doesn't have a place for us, then another world must be made. With no other tool than our rage, no other material than our dignity."[145]

The global vision and aspirations of Marcos and the Zapatistas were met with a fascination with them that was no less global in scale. Published translations of Marcos' writings and interviews exist in more than ten European languages, as well as several non-European ones (including Chinese, Indonesian, Japanese, Korean, Persian, Tamil and Turkish),[146] while Jorge Alonso claims that "with over 10,000 citations, he [i.e. Marcos] has also made a dent in the academic world."[147] What was it that so attracted the attention of the media, scholars, intellectuals, diverse political organizations, numerous social movements, and a host of social theorists and activists, to the Zapatista cause? How was a movement whose theatre of operations was limited, at least during its initial six years of public existence, to a single state in the Mexican Union (and then not even the entirety of Chiapas), able to attract such intense interest internationally, to the extent that it became a source of inspiration for so many? And, perhaps most crucially, how was Marcos, and through him the Zapatistas, able to translate this interest into inspiration for so many? What was the Subcomandante able to make them see in what was ostensibly a localized indigenous peasant movement that would prove inspirational to people around the globe?

Two scholars, each of whom has produced a book-length study in English on the international appeal of the Zapatistas, offer answers to these questions.[148] First, Thomas Olesen identifies several key factors explaining this phenomenon.[149] Some of these we can categorize as external to the Zapatistas themselves, being related to the ideas and attitudes circulating in the world at that time; whereas others can be interpreted as being intrinsic to the Zapatistas themselves, that is, their international appeal can be attributed to deliberate, conscious decisions made by Marcos and the movement as a whole. Taking the liberty of reordering and elaborating on the factors that Olesen cites, examples of the former category would include: (1) the fact that discontent toward neoliberalism, especially as espoused and prosecuted by Margaret Thatcher in the U.K. and Ronald Reagan in the U.S., already existed for the Zapatistas to tap into; and (2) the Left, having been demoralized by the recent ascendancy of neoliberalism and the demise of real existing socialism in the form of the Soviet Union and its satellite regimes in Eastern Europe, was in desperate need of new movement—preferably, I would stress, one that boasted a prominent and iconic figure on a par with Che Guevara—that they could place their faith and hope in. As for factors related to the second category, Olesen notes that: (1) the choice of the date of the Zapatista uprising to coincide with the coming into effect of NAFTA (and, I would add, Marcos' subsequent repeated stressing that this agreement was a trigger as it represented "a death sentence for the indigenous people"[150]), situated the Zapatista within a historical tradition of struggle against colonization of which NAFTA was merely the most current incarnation. Secondly, (2) the Zapatistas identify a common enemy, in the form of neoliberal economic globalization, for the Left to unite in opposition against—hence, although the exact details of the exploitation and suffering that people experience in each locale may differ, these are presented as having a common cause. Further, (3) the Zapatistas do not oppose globalization as such, and even less advocate a retreat into isolated and entrenched nationalism, but rather urge an alternative form of it than that which was currently being propagated (namely, I would urge, a diverse world in which people enjoy the autonomy necessary to live as they see fit, and not a homogenous (and homogenizing) one in which people are denied this). And lastly, (4) the Zapatistas repeatedly critiqued neoliberalism for being exclusionary and marginalizing while emphasizing their own commitment to democracy, especially in its radical, grassroots form. (Of course, as the Zapatistas' chief military strategist and spokesperson, Marcos, I would insist, played a preeminent role in formulating and articulating (1) - (4) above.)

Alex Khasnabish, who limits the focus of his study to the Zapatistas' appeal in North America, adds a further factor into the mix: resonance, which he explains "emerges from the capacity of people to be able to not simply adopt the struggles of Others but to connect with them, to make sense of them in ways that are not divorced from the contexts within which they live and work," and which "compels us to take issues of history, imagination, and context seriously."[151] Explaining the Zapatistas' resonance in North America, Khasnabish writes:

> An example of resistance; a thoughtful, democratic struggle for autonomy; a monumental gesture of defiance against the seemingly indomitable force of global neoliberal capitalism; a movement that cherishes life and laughter and connectedness; a demonstration of how tactics, strategies, and goals must always be considered in the context within which they are set and must always be subordinated to the will and the needs of the people they affect. These are but a few reasons why Zapatismo has

resonated so profoundly within activist communities
in the U.S. and Canada.[152]

Crucially, both Olesen and Khasnabish attribute to Marcos a "central role" in internationalizing the Zapatistas' appeal.[153] So too, both scholars highlight a novel aspect of the Zapatistas' interaction with sympathizers the world over: that they were able to transform what was initially a traditional relationship of one-way solidarity into a two-way, reciprocal, mutually beneficial dynamic.[154]

This last point is of great significance. Had the Zapatistas' limited their horizons to achieving local objectives (such as, for example, pressuring the Mexican government to grant autonomy for Chiapas' indigenous peoples), they would almost certainly still have garnered global attention and attracted peoples from all over the world to come and visit Zapatista territory and then further demonstrate their solidarity toward the Zapatista cause once they returned to their own countries. (After all, the Cuban government had managed to achieve such results.) However, the relationship would not have advanced beyond this. Instead, the Zapatistas, rather than merely inviting progressive forces the world over to support them in their struggle against neoliberal capitalist globalization, urge them to participate in this struggle by "customizing" the Zapatistas' experiences of resistance to fit local conditions. As the Subcomandante modestly phrased it: "We are just an experience…from which any other struggle may adopt or adapt whatever it finds useful for its own peculiar geographic conditions."[155]

In this way, the Zapatistas were able to inspire people the world over, not simply by being a symbol of resistance but by being something greater: a kind of school of resistance that showcases one possible way (among many) to resist neoliberal capitalist globalization. That the Zapatistas set about fulfilling their desire "to build…[a] gathering of rebellions, an exchange of learnings" (as Marcos puts it),[156] without ever adopting a high-handed attitude—but rather with the Subcomandante explicitly voicing their refusal to assume a vanguard role (with its temptation to hegemonize and homogenize)—has helped enhance their ability to inspire.[157]

Indeed, distinguished anthropologist Gary H. Gossen notes that "Zapatista models for consultative democracy and public policy are widely cited, from the streets of Brazil, Uruguay, and Argentina, to the legislative chambers of Venezuela and Bolivia," adding "Zapatismo, borne of local reality in Chiapas, has turned out to be a formative and highly influential voice in current Latin American politics."[158] So too, Naomi Klein observes how "This organizing model has spread throughout Latin America and the world," before specifically citing "the Landless Peasants' Movement of Brazil" and "the anarchist squats of Italy (called 'social centres')."[159]

In Europe, the Zapatistas proved especially inspirational in Italy. The Italian Communist Party and its youth league have both acknowledged the Zapatistas' influence on them. So too have Italian radical left activists such as the Ya Basta Association, which is a network of anti-capitalist and pro-immigrant-rights organizations, and its offshoot, the White Overalls, who champion rights for precarious workers such as those with non-fixed employment contracts.[160] However, the Zapatistas' impact was not limited to Western Europe: they similarly provided those living on Europe's eastern-most border with a point of reference and a source of inspiration. The Russian collective Chto Delat (What is to be done?), established in 2003 in Petersburg by a group of artists, critics, philosophers, and writers from several major Russian cities who seek to blend art, activism, and political theory, notes how:

> the publication of Russian translations of texts by the Zapatistas and Subcomandante Marcos...opened a different dimension of politics to the apolitical Russian intelligentsia for the first time, revealing its

connections with poetics and the ideas of radical democracy.... These texts became the basis for the appearance of new left forces in Russia and at that moment, Russia's marginalized grass-roots politics turned out to synchronize with worldwide tendencies in which the declarations and positions of Zapatism played a crucial role.... [T]oday, when we must look for new paths of resistance and struggle, their experience is again becoming vital for us. We once again seek to see ourselves in relation to the ideas of Zapatism, understand what processes are taking place in indigenous communities and measure whether we can apply them in our own lives and struggle.[161]

The Zapatistas also impacted greatly on political activism in the U.S. and Canada. Khasnabish was able to interview more than thirty activists from over ten different organizations and projects in North America "who had experienced the resonance of Zapatismo and translated it in ways that were meaningful and powerful within the socio-political and cultural contexts where they live and work."[162] Some of these organizations centred on the Zapatista movement itself, but some had a broader focus, such as on the state of Chiapas or on Mexico in general, and still others located their primary focus elsewhere than Mexico or had a much wider focus.[163] Especially illustrative is the case of the activist media makers Big Noise Tactical, one of whose founding members, Rick Rowley, explained to Khasnabish how BNT originated:

we all accepted that invitation to become Zapatistas and we returned [from visiting Mexico] to the United States as Zapatistas looking for what that might mean in the north and trying to learn from their example of struggle...not just as an inspiration but to learn from their tactics and their strategy.... [W]e thought video made sense as a language that could circulate through these circuits of American culture.... We've never thought of ourselves as film makers but as Zapatistas looking for forms of struggle that make sense in the north.[164]

Finally, scholar Thomas Nail, after noting that "The intersectional analysis of power, prefiguration, participatory politics, and horizontalism are four of the most defining characteristics of revolutionary struggles of the last 20 years," continues: "The appearance of these tactics in the Alter-Globalization Movement, the World Social Forum, [Spain's anti-austerity movement] the *Indignados*, the Occupy Movement, and much of contemporary radical organizing, can all be traced back to the influence and inspiration of the Zapatistas in the early 90s."[165]

The result has been that through the efforts of their Subcomandante, the Zapatistas, by listening to and validating others' experiences and practices of resistance while simultaneously encouraging them to take from the Zapatista struggle whatever is useful for their own struggles in their own locales, have helped weave a web of resistance to neoliberal capitalist globalization. Indeed, Marcos had outlined his vision for doing precisely this as early as the August 1996 International Encuentro Against Neoliberalism and For Humanity, when he declared,

[W]e will make a collective network of all our particular struggles and resistances, an intercontinental network of resistance against neoliberalism, an intercontinental network of resistance for humanity. This intercontinental network of resistance, recognizing differences and acknowledging similarities, will strive to find itself in other resistances around the world. This intercontinental network of resistance will be the medium in which distinct resistances may support one another.... [166]

As it would turn out, the 1996 Zapatista Encuentro proved a hugely inspirational event and marked a milestone in the development of the alter-globalization movement.[167] As Paul Kingsnorth observes,

> It created the key corridor down which the ideas and principles of *Zapatismo* began to inspire and create a global movement of political resistance...[and] sent *Zapatismo* global. The 3,000 delegates returned to their countries with new ideas, new ways of thinking about the future, and above all, new links. The next year, another Encuentro was held, this time in Spain, which would cement those links even further. From it, more than any other single event before or since, would grow the "anti-globalisation" movement as it exists today.[168]

For one thing, it inspired the founding of Peoples' Global Action, which very much aspired to being the network that Marcos had called for in his speech above. PGA constituted a web of grassroots social movements created by 300 people hailing from more than 70 countries who sought to connect their struggles by building equal, non-hierarchical relationships so as to resist neoliberal capitalist globalization through civil disobedience and non-violent direct action. Its principles involved a rejection of domination and discrimination (in all their forms) and the embracing of diversity and human dignity, while its organizational philosophy was founded on decentralization, horizontalism (meaning non-hierarchical decision-making processes and practices), and autonomy.[169] Clearly, these bear a striking resemblance to the Zapatistas' own ethics and practice, and not without good reason. Ultimately, as Kingsnorth makes clear,

PGA took the new political forms, the new ideas about power and the new methods of makings things happen that had come out of Chiapas, and ran with them on a global scale. The result was events like [the summit protests in] Seattle, Prague, Genoa – and the global movement we have today. For it was PGA...in the role of inspiration and key player...[that] helped create the kind of "take on a big summit" action that came to define the first stage of the anti-globalisation movement.[170]

Indeed, more generally, Khasnabish has noted how, "the alter-globalisation movement's commitment to direct action, deep sense of inclusiveness rather than sectarianism, espousal of a 'diversity of tactics,' and radical spirit of socio-political change that does not aim to claim power over others in order to transform the world, can all be traced in large part to the Zapatistas."[171]

The transnational appeal of the Zapatistas among scholars, activists, social movements, political groups, rights organizations, and progressive forces, lay in their possessing a global vision that was not limited to bringing about merely another indigenous politics, or even another national politics, but rather another politics completely. Such a politics was based on new values, visions, principles, and practices for a new age: namely, diversity, collectivism, autonomy, horizontality in social relations, decentralized organizational structures, communal decision-making, and radical grassroots democracy. The Zapatistas had extracted and distilled these from their intense, prolonged and hard-won experience of real, lived struggle: as indigenous peoples resisting half a millennium of colonial exploitation; as Chiapan peasants organizing politically to oppose the inroads of neoliberal capitalist globalization; and (under Marcos) as clandestine rural guerrillas confronting state repression and violence at the hands of local landowning elites. Through their Subcomandante, the Zapatistas now offered up to a newly emerging global civil society these key elements of Zapatismo, which were universally relevant and applicable, and therefore readily translatable to struggles elsewhere, regardless of their particular contexts.

Significantly, this new politics practiced by the Zapatistas— and which through their subcomandante-spokesperson they proffered to the world—was "other" in that it broke with the politics espoused by the old armed revolutionary Left. True, Zapatismo drew inspiration from, and retained the spirit of, the militant Left of old, an inheritance Marcos brought with him to the Zapatista movement, as the Subcomandante makes clear:

> We are going to try to construct, or reconstruct, another way of doing politics, one that once again has the spirit of serving others, without material interests, with sacrifice, with dedication, with honesty, which keeps its word, whose sole payment is the satisfaction of duty fulfilled; that is, like the militants of the Left did before, who were not stopped by blows, jail or death, much less by dollar bills.[172]

However, while recalling this spirit, the Zapatistas' "other" politics did not represent merely the resurrection or rehabilitation of those militant politics; rather, it involved their considerable renovation. As the Subcomandante would tell one interviewer, "The old recipes or the old parameters should serve as a reference, yes, of what was done, but not as something that should be re-adopted to do something new."[173] Instead, Marcos has repeatedly distanced himself and the Zapatistas from their predecessors among the armed revolutionary Left. For example, he told Gabriel García Márquez that,

> The world in general, and Mexican society in particular, is composed of different kinds of people, and the relations between them have to be founded on respect and tolerance, things which appear

in none of the discourses of the politico-military organizations of the sixties and seventies.[174]

In another interview he stated,

> If your tendency is to become a mass-based army [as ours is], then you can't put so much emphasis on the old, traditional vertical guerrilla discipline – the you're-with-us-or-you-are-dead school of thought. You can't raise the step so high that nobody can climb it; you have to make room for all the people to participate to the best of their abilities, and so you are always in the process of looking for what unites people, and not what separates – what adds, and not what not subtracts. That is why we are not...a guerrilla force: we are an army with a flag wide enough to embrace everyone.... [175]

And in a February 1995 communiqué Marcos again highlighted the contrast between the EZLN and other guerrilla groups, asking rhetorically,

> What other guerrilla force has appealed, not to the proletariat as the historical vanguard, but to the civic society that struggles for democracy? What other guerrilla force has stepped aside in order not to interfere in the electoral process? What other guerrilla force has convened a national democratic movement, civic and peaceful, so that armed struggle becomes useless? What other guerrilla force asks its bases of support about what it should do before doing it? What other guerrilla force has struggled to achieve a democratic space and not take power? What other guerrilla force has relied more on words than on bullets?[176]

Perhaps the key factor that allowed the Zapatistas to come up with "another politics" was their being the first post-communist armed left-wing movement, meaning that they were not driven by an overarching Marxist or Maoist ideology. This had important implications. First, it liberated them from certain Leninist constraints; most notably, a preoccupation with seizing state power, and a perception of themselves as constituting a revolutionary vanguard. As Marcos declared,

> We do not want a revolution imposed from the top: it always turns against itself. We are not a vanguard.[177] We are not here to close things down but to start [to] renew our efforts.... Our aim: to give voice to civil society, everywhere, under all its forms, in all its fronts. We are neither the only ones nor the best ones. We do not have the truth or the answer to everything. Provided we raise good questions, that is enough for us.[178]

Indeed, this freedom from Leninist dogma enabled the Zapatistas to approach the question of power in a different way. As the Subcomandante stated in a 1996 speech,

> [W]e believe that the problem of power must be redefined, not repeating the formula that in order to change the world it is necessary to take power and, once in power, then we are going to organize things in the best interest of the world, that is, in my own best interest since I am in power. We have thought that if we were to conceive of a change of premise in looking at power, the problem of power, explaining that we did not want to seize it, this was going to produce another form of politics.... [179]

Secondly, it meant that, unlike the old armed revolutionary Left, the Zapatistas did not seek to export their own unique brand of revolution worldwide or implant a dogmatic ideology in every country irrespective of local conditions. On the contrary, Marcos specifically states in one interview: "We are a...point of reference. But not...a model to follow. We say to...those who follow our example, don't follow it. We think everyone has to build his or her own experience and not repeat models...don't try to export Zapatismo or import it."[180] After all, as Marcos has made clear, Zapatismo is an intuition, not an ideology,[181] even less some Soviet or Chinese Socialist template that must be rigidly adhered to and strictly implemented regardless of the various social realities it encounters. Instead, Marcos and the Zapatistas saw their role as extending an invitation to people everywhere to take from the Zapatista experience whatever ideas and practices they feel they can effectively use or customize to confront and resist neoliberal capitalist globalization in their own locales and contexts.

Finally, unconstrained by rigid Marxist dogma, the Zapatistas could free themselves from having to privilege the class struggle to the extent that all other struggles—most notably those involving championing the rights of indigenous peoples, women, and the LGBTQ community—were subsumed by it. Indeed, eminent sociologist and world-systems analyst Immanuel Wallerstein argues that the Zapatistas "are part of a post-1968 view that the traditional analyses of the Old Left were too narrow, in that they seemed to emphasize only the problems and struggles of the urban industrial proletariat," adding that "The Zapatistas are proclaiming that the struggle for rights of *every* oppressed group is equally important, and the struggle must be fought on all fronts at the same time."[182] To illustrate this point, Wallerstein points out that during a Zapatista-convened colloquium that he attended and at which the Subcomandante gave seven presentations, "Marcos devoted one whole talk to the struggles of women for their rights...[and] devoted another to the crucial importance of control of the land by the world's rural workers." Significantly, in his fifth presentation at the colloquium Marcos stated:

Claiming that the core of capitalist domination lies in the ownership of the means of production does not mean that we ignore or are unaware of other spaces of domination. It is clear to us that transformations must not focus only on material conditions. That's why for us there is no hierarchy of spheres; we do not claim that the fight for land has priority over the gender struggle, nor that the gender struggle is more important than the fight to recognize and respect difference. Instead, we think that all types of emphasis are necessary.... [183]

Six years earlier, the Subcomandante had highlighted the contrast between the Zapatistas and the old Marxist Left in this respect, noting how,

> homosexuals, lesbians, transsexuals...were not simply excluded by the discourses of the Latin America Left of those decades – and still current today – but the theoretical framework of what was then Marxism-Leninism disregarded them, indeed took them to be part of the front to be eliminated. Homosexuals, for example, were suspect as potential traitors, elements harmful to the socialist movement and state. While the indigenous peoples were viewed as a backward sector preventing the forces of production...blah, blah, blah.[184]

The Zapatistas' refusal to relegate or subordinate other struggles (e.g. for land, for indigenous people's rights, for women's rights, and for LGBTQ rights) not only represents a shift away from the class-based politics of the Old Left and towards "another politics" based on identity, but also explains the movement's broad appeal. Marcos, having noted that "Since the beginning of our uprising... we received, and fortunately continue to receive, support...from indigenous people, from women, from young people, and from gays, lesbians, transgender people, transsexuals," then attributed this as being "because we have in common the status of being 'others,' excluded, discriminated against, feared."[185]

In short, the "other" politics proposed and practiced by the Zapatistas differed markedly from that of the old armed revolutionary Left: in place of an ideology, "an intuition"[186]; in place of dogmatism, diversity of opinion; in place of rigid thought, flexible thinking; in place of imposing one's will, building consensus; in place of a single solution, a plurality of possibilities; in place of hegemony, horizontality; in place of Marxist orthodoxy, post-Marxist heterodoxy; in place of a Communist International, an "International of Hope"; in place of a class-based politics, a politics based on identity; in place of a distorted communism, a true collectivism; in place of seizing power, "build[ing] a new relationship between power and citizens"[187]; in place of seizing the reins of the state, a "radical change of all the social relations in today's Mexico"[188]; and in place of "think[ing] that things can be transformed from above...think[ing] that society, and the world, should be transformed from below."[189]

However, while the Zapatistas' politics is distinctly different from the old armed revolutionary Latin American Left, especially in that it does not reduce revolutionary politics to armed struggle against the State, it nonetheless remains decidedly revolutionary. For one thing, it aims not only at bringing about radical political and social change from below, but also, as Marcos makes clear, at "revolutionizing political power...changing fundamentally the form of doing politics."[190] For another, Marcos notes, the Zapatistas themselves continue to firmly believe that "A profound and radical change of all the social relations in today's Mexico is necessary. A REVOLUTION IS NECESSARY, a new revolution."[191] Significantly too, they have remained armed, refusing to put down their weapons, although they have not fired them in anger since January 1994, and have also consistently rejected becoming part of the institutional or electoral Left, declining to endorse any political party, let alone join or become one.

In this way, they have shunned two paths that have been trodden by so many of the armed revolutionary Latin American Left of old: embracing reformism and joining the institutional Left (as did a slew of former left-wing guerrillas who became politicians[192]); or capitulating completely, repudiating their previous left-wing principles and taking up capitalism (and sometimes even government posts). Instead, the "other" politics pursued by the Zapatistas remains steadfastly anti-capitalist, while being, nonetheless, inclusive, undogmatic, non-hegemonic, decentralized, radically democratic, and not exclusively class-based. Marcos, in particular, has consistently articulated a devastating critique of capitalism employing the Marxist analytical framework and critical tools furnished by his Marxist formation both at university and in the underground revolutionary guerrilla organization, the Forces of National Liberation.

Over a period of many years, and in numerous communiqués, speeches and presentations, the Subcomandante, drawing to some extent on Marx's analytical framework and utilizing certain core concepts from *Capital*, as well as contributing his own arguments, has offered a searing critique of capitalism.[193] For instance, he charges it with: concentrating wealth in the hands of a few, predominantly through exploiting and plundering the many; repressing anyone who rebels against such exploitation and dispossession; holding up exploiters and plunderers as figures to be admired and imitated, instead of holding them to account; bringing about the commodification of absolutely everything, including people, nature (both the resources it yields, such as gas and oil, but also, to feed the tourist industry, its beauty), ancestral knowledge, genetic codes, water, air, culture, history, and consciences; wreaking environmental destruction and exacerbating natural disasters through commodifying natural resources and prioritizing profits over preservation; destroying nation states and national (and cultural) identities— since these stand in the way of the transnational movement of capital specifically and neoliberal economic globalization more generally—so as to reconstruct them according to a single model; and finally, promoting fear of the "other."

The Subcomandante has also striven to dispel one of the major myths associated with capitalism: namely, that the free market goes hand-in-hand with peace. On the contrary, he argues, war is not merely connected to capitalism, it is essential to it. In addition to war being an industry in itself, and one that generates massive profits, it is through war that capitalism imposes itself on territories that have thus far remained outside the capitalist world economy, exploiting the labour and raw materials located in them, producing new commodities from these resources, and transforming these "peripheral" areas into potential new markets.[194]

Importantly however, while elaborating these critiques of capitalism, Marcos also voices his vehement opposition to the idea, bandied around in leftist circles, that capitalism is in its death-throes, its self-destruction assured and imminent, and that what needs to be concentrated on now is what follows on from capitalism. Instead, the Subcomandante insists that capitalism remains "fully functional and prosperous," that it still "exploits us, dispossesses us, represses us, despises us," and that it is even becoming "more powerful, cruel and bloodthirsty."[195] Moreover, he goes further, outlining what he believes to be an effective means of combatting capitalism. This involves waging a collective and organized struggle, and more precisely, forming "a broad movement...from the entire spectrum of anti-capitalist opposition," that "does not...ignore...other spaces of domination...[and] must not focus only on material conditions," nor even relegate to secondary importance the struggle for indigenous, LGBTQ, and women's rights, and that seeks to "confront and defeat its [i.e. capitalism's] core: private ownership of the means of production and exchange."[196] More recently, the Subcomandante has stressed that this "organized struggle from below...must enlist as support...critical thought."[197]

In offering up this sustained and detailed analytical attack on capitalism, and by affording strategies for opposing and destroying it, Marcos and his fellow Zapatistas have shown their refusal to embrace defeatism and resignation. Voicing their utter rejection of the assertion, made into mantra by Margaret Thatcher, that "There Is No Alternative," they urge instead that things can, and indeed have to be, different. The alternative, one could almost say "antidote," to neoliberal capitalist globalization that they propose lies in the concept and practice of autonomy.

For the Zapatistas, autonomy involves the creation of social spaces where indigenous peoples are free to express their ethnic identity by living according to their own customs and practices. This means that they administer and govern themselves economically, politically, judicially, and culturally, establishing their own forms of organization and exercising sovereignty over their land, its resources (including subsoil ones), and how it is used (namely through the collective ownership and management of the land). The Zapatistas describe how they came to realise

> that it was necessary to build our life ourselves, with autonomy...[and] we began to form our own system of governing—our autonomy—with our own education system, our own health care, our own communication, our way of caring for and working on mother earth; our own politics as a people and our own ideology about how we want to live as communities, with an other culture.[198]

Contrary to what some critics have claimed, this does not, however, represent a call for separatism, as Marcos has made clear: "The EZLN and the entire national indigenous movement do not want Indian peoples to separate themselves from Mexico: they intend to be recognized as an integral part of the country, but with their own particularities."[199] What this call for self-government and self-administration *has* translated into, over time, is autonomy in the provisioning of healthcare and education, the dispensing of justice, the practicing of agro-ecology, the establishing of cooperatives producing certain goods (e.g. boots and coffee), and the setting up of financial banks.

The Subcomandante, in relating "[t]he starting point for [the Zapatistas'] advances in government, health, education, housing, nutrition, women's participation, trade, culture, communication, and information," points to the implementation in Zapatista territory of the EZLN's Revolutionary Agrarian Law (December 1993), which emphasised the collective ownership of property, the collective working of land, collective administration, the instilling of a collective consciousness, and the establishment of rural collectives.[200] Thus, Zapatista autonomy is fundamentally built on collectivism, which entails conducting politics through communal decision-making practices, with the ultimate result that social relations are no longer mediated by the capitalist state.

Moreover, and crucially, autonomy as envisaged by the Zapatistas is not a state of being but a process; it is something that, rather than being an achieved end, is to be constantly practiced. And this practice is guided by the Zapatistas' seven principles of command-by-obeying: (1) to serve, not self-serve; (2) to represent, not supplant; (3) to construct, not destroy; (4) to obey, not command; (5) to propose, not impose; (6) to convince, not conquer; and (7) to go below, not rise above.[201] In keeping with these principles, the men and women who are chosen by their communities to serve on the five Good Government Committees (at the zone level), on the autonomous councils (at the municipal level), and on local commissions (at the community level), do so unpaid, are regularly rotated, and can be recalled from their posts by the communities that they serve if deemed to be carrying out their duties unsatisfactorily.[202] As one pair of commentators has noted, this "prevents the professionalization of political participation and the formation of a political class… and precludes the attachment of authority to a position of delegated responsibility."[203] Pertinently, Marcos has stressed the fact that those who serve the Zapatista autonomous communities by carrying out the work of governing are not "professional politicians" and yet they appear to serve their constituents better than the latter:

> [I]t turns out that this work [of governing Zapatista communities] not only is unpaid, it is also not considered a specialty. In other words, someone who is [an] autonomous municipal president one day was in the fields the day before, or on the coffee plantation, planting or harvesting. Many of our Zapatista leaders did not even go to school or do not even know how to speak Spanish; in other words, they are not specialists in anything, much less in politics. And, nonetheless, our autonomous municipalities have more advances in health, education, housing, and nutrition than the official municipalities that are governed by professional politicians, by political specialists.[204]

More than merely representing something that is being built on the ground in Chiapas however, Zapatista autonomy has wider significance: if interpreted as a broad political-philosophical principle and practice, it is something that can be adopted and utilized by others who are confronting neoliberal capitalist globalization elsewhere in the world. After all, Zapatista autonomy fundamentally challenges the conventional and entrenched notion that "government equals the capitalist state," and indeed seeks to render the state irrelevant, bypassing its apparatus, branches, and institutions. As Alvaro Reyes has put it, "the primary effect [of these 'non-state forms of government'] is the practical annihilation of the state structure...through the institutionalization of unrestricted mass political participation, that is, self-government." Reyes calls this a "recovery of government from the clutches of the capitalist state" that marks "the key contribution of the Zapatistas...for an anti-capitalist left."[205] And, on an ethical as opposed to purely political level—because Zapatista autonomy is in essence based on collectivism—it represents the antithesis of the rampant individualism that both underpins and in turn is promoted by capitalism.

This explains why the Zapatistas have been so keen to showcase their experience of building autonomy in Chiapas. This they have done through a series of initiatives, one of which was "the 'Zapatista Little School,' a series of residential experiences in Zapatista communities inaugurated in 2013 for those who wanted to learn about Zapatista autonomy and think about how such ideas and practices might apply in their own contexts."[206] As Marcos told a gathering of the Zapatistas' supporters at the August 2008 National and International Caravan for Observation and Solidarity with Zapatista Communities: "We want...you... to understand directly what is happening with...the process of building autonomy within the Zapatista communities" so that "a relationship between compañeros is established...[a] gathering of rebellions, an exchange of learnings, and a more direct relationship...of support." Hence Reyes' conclusion that "For the Zapatistas then, 'autonomy'...is an explicitly universalizable practice."[207]

Ultimately therefore, the Zapatistas' "other" politics, through its vehement anti-capitalism and its emphasis on autonomy—one could say, its proposing substituting the accumulation of capital for the accumulation of autonomy—constitutes an alternative to retreat, repudiation, renunciation, and reformism, and as such, offers a way forward for the global Left. Returning to the Subcomandante specifically, what can we say about his role in helping to bring about another world than the one that exists today? Of course, there are his constant and indefatigable efforts at promoting autonomy and the compelling anti-capitalist critique that he has offered up to the world. However, his true significance lies in his being an iconic rallying figure, not just for the armed revolutionary Left, but also, and more importantly, for the global Left more generally, as well as for an emerging alter-globalization movement, and for progressive forces the world over. The performance artist, activist and author Guillermo Gómez-Peña offers a partial explanation for the Subcomandante's exceedingly broad appeal, writing,

> In the confusing era of "the end of ideology," his [i.e. Marcos'] utopian political visions of a multiracial, multigendered, multiparticipatory Mexico—presented in simple, non-ideological, and poetic language—went straight to the jaded hearts and minds of students, activists, intellectuals, artists, nihilistic teens, and even apolitical middle-class professionals. In an era of ferocious neo-nationalisms, he made sure to avoid separatist jargon and dogmas. His combination of political clarity, bravado, and humility seduced progressive politicians and activists throughout the world. His eclectic discourse, spiced with irreverent humor and an array of surprising references to pop culture, contemporary writers and topical world news, revealed a sophisticated internationalism.[208]

If we dissect the Subcomandante's appeal among certain constituencies, then, for the revolutionary armed Left, which had been bereft of a charismatic icon for almost a generation, the Subcomandante—gun-in-hand and with his Maoist cap, Guevaran pipe, and bandoliers criss-crossing his chest in imitation of Mexican revolutionary Emiliano Zapata—represented an obvious successor to Che Guevara, who had been executed in Bolivia in 1967.

As for the global Left, by the time 1994 had dawned much of it was largely shattered and broken.[209] Britain had endured more than a decade of Thatcherism, which entailed economic restructuring, privatization, and cutting back on social services and welfare spending—what one could accurately call a war on the poor—as well as the message, repeatedly hammered home, that There Is No Alternative to free-market capitalism. In the U.S., the 1980s had been dominated by a similar phenomenon: Reaganomics. Marcos' own take on the situation, both generally and in Mexico specifically, was that,

> The socialist bloc had been defeated, the entire left-wing movement in Latin America was in a period of retreat. In Mexico, the Left was sobbing about defeat after [President] Salinas de Gortari not only had committed [electoral] fraud, but also had bought a good part of the Mexican Left's critical conscience.[210]

What is more, the five-year period prior to Marcos' debut on the world stage had seen the Fall of the Berlin Wall; the disintegration of the Soviet Union, the primary example (albeit a very imperfect one) of actually existing socialism; the voting-out-of-power of the Sandinistas in Nicaragua; and left-wing guerrilla groups in El Salvador, Ecuador, and Colombia putting down their weapons and entering into peace negotiations with their respective governments. Globally, neoliberalism was in its ascendancy and indeed appeared unstoppable. With the demise of so-called "actual existing socialism" in the form of the Soviet bloc, the most compelling alternative (ideological and concrete) to neoliberal capitalism was gone.

In the face of this neoliberal onslaught, which exhibited a marked triumphalism—"the end of history" and "There Is No Alternative" having both been declared—the global Left suffered a deep-seated crisis of identity and confidence, and had become distinctly demoralized. Some recanted their Marxism and embraced the new order, others simply became disillusioned and withdrew into despondency. Indeed, in an October 1994 communiqué, Marcos, after noting that recently those on the Left appeared to lack "the desire to fight," asked rhetorically if this was "Because of the moral hangover after the collapse of the socialist camp? A tactical 'retreat' in the face of the overwhelming force of the 'marine boys' and neoliberalism? The 'end of history?'" He continued:

> What happened to them [i.e. those on the Left]?... Did they get tired? Did they get bored? Did they sell out? Did they surrender? Wasn't it worth it? Isn't it worth it?... I see that now cynicism is the flag of the Left. "Realism," a columnist will correct me, "realpolitik," another will add.[211]

The Subcomandante appeared then precisely when a deflated and demoralized global Left was flagging and in most dire need of a rallying figure. The effect of his appearance was to give those on the Left a shot in the arm, to act as a morale booster as it were.

As for the alter-globalists, Marcos appeared just as this nascent movement was beginning to form, and in doing so, provided it with an eloquent, instantly recognizable, iconic figure around which to coalesce.[212] Moreover, and importantly, as Andrew Jones points out, the Subcomandante constitutes "one of the leading radical thinkers on globalization from the Global South."[213]

Finally, as for progressive forces the world over, in an age when most people no longer self-identified as proletarians, self-proclaimed Marxism-Leninist revolutionaries enjoyed extremely limited appeal, whereas, by contrast, with the dawning of an era of anti-racism and pro-indigenous rights—1993 was the UN's International Year for the World's Indigenous Peoples—Marcos, who championed the indigenous cause and has fought against all forms of social exclusion and discrimination, has enjoyed broad-based appeal. Indeed, being untainted by any association with gulags, purges, and repression—as were, in many people's eyes, the Maoist or Marxist-Leninist revolutionaries of yesteryear—and by rejecting the label of "political revolutionary," preferring instead that of "social rebel,"[214] preaching democracy not dictatorship of the proletariat, favouring the pen over the sword, and distancing himself from the anti-intellectualism that had traditionally afflicted much of the armed revolutionary Left, the Subcomandante has been able to garner widespread support among a cross-section of progressive global society.

Undoubtedly, Marcos' appeal was supplemented too, in part, by his self-sacrifice, and in particular the moral authority that attends him as someone who had abandoned a comfortable middle-class urban lifestyle as an academic in favour of enduring the hardships of a rural guerrilla existence championing indigenous peasants who are rebelling against government neglect, racism, and repression. After all, Marcos could not have known during those ten long, lonely years of living a largely isolated and itinerant existence devoid of creature comforts in the desolation of Chiapas' mountains that he would become an icon; he had, on the contrary, run the very real risk of dying in obscurity from disease, violence, or snake bite, as had so many indigenous Chiapan peasants, and not a few Latin American guerrillas. Indeed, the Subcomandante's sharing in the harsh living conditions of Chiapas' indigenous peasantry, but also, and especially, his living strictly in accordance with the values he espouses, lends him a profoundly ethical hue. This perhaps explains why Naomi Klein, in a piece on the Subcomandante titled "The Unknown Icon," claimed that "Marcos is the descendant of [Martin Luther] King, Che Guevara, Malcom X, Emiliano Zapata and all the other heroes who preached from pulpits only to be shot down one by one" adding, "[i]n their place, the world now has a new kind of hero, one who listens more than speaks, who preaches in riddles not in certainties, a leader who doesn't show his face, who says his mask is really a mirror."[215] Similarly, Algerian-born French political-philosopher, professor, and columnist Sami Naïr described Marcos as "a hybrid...character: a kind of Che-Gandhi," arguing that the Subcomandante had managed to unite "the moral rejection of violence [that] proceeded in Gandhi from absolute respect for all life" with what "for Che had the same moral profundity, risking dying for the liberation of life."[216] Finally, the eminent U.S. sociologist and Yale scholar Immanuel

Wallerstein situates Marcos within a pantheon of "world moral heroes" that include Gandhi and Mandela.

It is important to note that, with the exception of Marcos, all those listed by Klein, Naïr, and Wallerstein are no longer with us, meaning that the Subcomandante may well be the sole surviving globally recognized (and recognizable) ethical hero of iconic stature. At the very least, if we consider (as we surely must) the Subcomandante to be a political figure, one is forced to ask if there is any other current candidate within this category who enjoys comparable appeal; that is charismatic, admirable, and inspires trust on account of their self-sacrifice, integrity, and the fact that they consistently practice what they preach.[217] More to the point, how many prominent political figures in the world today have demonstrated a preparedness either to die for what they believe in or to live in complete accordance with the ethics they espouse, let alone to do both?

In 1994, Mexico's President Salinas, not without a degree of hypocrisy given his government's track record on violent repression,[218] branded the Subcomandante a "professional of violence," to which Marcos retorted that he was rather a "professional of hope." History will judge the accuracy of the Subcomandante's self-styled epithet.

Appendix:
Subcomandante Marcos' Communiqué

In (Self-)Defense of Giraffes[1]

---

[1] The Spanish original can be found online at: https://bit.ly/2TIS2zZ. I am extremely grateful to Henry Gales, an experienced translator of Marcos and Zapatista texts (http://galestranslations.blogspot.com), for his assistance and advice regarding the translation that follows. Needless to say, any defects or deficiencies are entirely my responsibility.

FOREWORD

I have chosen to produce a translation of this communiqué and to include it here for two reasons. First, it is emblematic of the Subcomandante's overall message, meaning that it is anti-neoliberal capitalist globalization and pro-social inclusion (i.e. it is against all forms of discrimination), while also being highly reflective of the postmodern style he employs when communicating this message (i.e. it incorporates references to both "high" and "popular" culture, and displays irony and parody, to produce a text that is a pastiche). In short, it is thus quintessential Marcos. Secondly, it is one of those few communiqués by the Subcomandante that seems to have fallen through the cracks, with no English translation appearing either online or in the numerous edited collections of Subcomandante Marcos' works that have been published.

IN (SELF-)DEFENSE OF GIRAFFES

I. First, a Brief, but Necessary, Profile of Giraffes

Giraffe. An animal of great stature. It can reach a height of 5.3 meters. It is the tallest animal. It lives in dry regions with scattered woodland, south of the Sahara Desert. Giraffes, females and males, are endowed with two or four short, blunt horns, covered with skin. A giraffe's coat exhibits spots of dark hair on a creamy background, the perfect camouflage among the ensemble of light and shade of the dense foliage. Giraffes rest and sleep while standing. Communication between giraffes is carried out through the emission of moans and other sounds involving very low notes. Giraffes defend themselves by kicking.

II. A Neoliberal Trick: "Destiny" for Those Above, "Freedom" for Those Below

On the great global television, channel one, the only and eternal [channel of] neoliberalism, presents an image repeated *ad nauseam*: the rich are rich owing to destiny, god or inheritance (as the case may be); and, on the other hand, the poor are poor because they want to be poor.

Thus, the rich must suffer the dictatorship of fate and "endure," unable to oppose it, a lifetime of luxury and impunity (although, technically speaking, impunity is also a luxury); while the poor enjoy the freedom to choose to be poor, and do not have to subject themselves to anything…because they have nothing.

Neoliberalism proposes, during primetime, one globalization above and another below. Above, wealth is presented, less like on a television screen and more like in a fish tank. The fish are beautiful, yes, but they are prisoners behind the glass. Below, poverty is presented as the freedom to choose between being below or above....

However, this is the same old story that is drummed into us, in many ways and at all times: "You cannot be like us (fate has reserved for us the right of admission). But, instead, you have the freedom to try to look like us. You can choose to dress like us, skin color is secondary if it is covered with brand clothing. You can choose to sing, dance, make love like us. But above all, you must choose to think like us." In short, slavery disguised as "induced freedom."

III. When Power Defines the "Other," it Defines the Enemy

As never before, the cornerstones of this crime against humanity called "capitalism" are laid in every corner of the planet: those who produce wealth are "liberated" from everything that is not their production capacity. And the modern global *Operation Freedom* now has military and financial means that are several times greater than the "liberating" capacity of the atomic bombs dropped on Hiroshima and Nagasaki.

The strange alchemy of the globalization of those above has achieved the globalization of a new dogma: the liberation of humanity is the same as the liberation of markets. All over the planet and in all languages, the new prayer is repeated and a new god is worshipped, which, like all the previous ones, is capricious, unstable and incomprehensible: the market.

And, like the previous gods, the market does not stride forth with the rationality of figures, statistics, laws of supply and demand, financial calculations. No, this new god has footsteps of death and destruction, of war.

Nor will it admit that it destroys; rather, it distributes, democratically, homogeneity with a swinging back and forth between limited identities: buyer-seller. Everything, but above all, all those who cannot or do not want to be one or the other of these, to keep time with the shrill and frenetic beat of the market, are "others."

Nor will it recognize that it kills; rather, it "humanizes" by imposing an order that "repopulates" the face of the earth: the order of its hegemony. Those who do not comply with that order, are "others." The new "truth" is not so new....

> The Indians, victims of the most gigantic dispossession in world history, continue to suffer the usurpation of the last remnants of their lands, and continue to be condemned to having their distinct identity negated.... In the beginning, the plundering and the *othercide* was carried out in the name of the God of heaven. Now, these are conducted in the name of the god of Progress.

(Eduardo Galeano, *Ser como ellos* [*To Be Like Them*])

If before, the "others" were the Indians, the blacks, the yellows or the reds, now globalization from above has brought us an authentic "global democratization": the "others" are everyone, and EVERY ONE of us who does not want to be like the hegemonic model, and refuses to homogenize our identity; that is, who resists renouncing our difference.

It is in difference, in recognizing it, in attempting to understand it, that is, to respect it, that the basis of humanity lies. By defining those who are different as the enemy, Power defines the whole of humanity as an opponent to annihilate.

IV. The New World Order in Short: Rich Countries Are So at the Expense of Poor Countries

Neoliberal modernity has also modernized language: where before there was talk of "gallows," now there is talk of "servicing foreign debt." It sounds better, but it's more lethal.

On the great globalized television, the poor countries produce wealth, and the rich countries produce financial institutions that collect this wealth.

Mexico, which is a poor country, has paid in the last ten years almost $350 billion for what is called "servicing foreign debt." As far as the government "of change" goes,[2] it has spent annually about six times more on "servicing the debt" than what has been spent on combating poverty over the same period.

Of the total paid by Mexico, which is a poor country, over the last ten years, a quarter has been to the World Bank, the International Monetary Fund and the Inter-American Development Bank (which, either are not poor, or keep up appearances well), and close to two thirds has been to banks from rich countries (mostly from the United States, and to a lesser extent European, Japanese, Canadian and Asian banks).

Latin America, which is a region of poor countries, for each dollar that it receives in loans, pays back eight and is left owing four. The creditors? American and European banks (mainly English, French and Spanish).

In short, the globalization of above has simplified geography: in the world there is no longer North and South, East and West, now there are countries that pay and countries that collect. And not only that, if before the "law" was "he who pays is in charge" now it is a case of "he who collects is in charge."

---

[2] This was a label attached to the government of Vicente Fox; the "change" referred to the change of government from the Institutional Revolutionary Party, which had held power for more than seven decades, to the National Action Party.

But the new god has, like the previous ones, feet of clay. Its primary driving force is not the generation of wealth, but financial speculation.

The neoliberal market, fascinated by the frenetic comings and goings of capital (the ubiquity of financial capital, a miracle produced by information superhighways), has "forgotten" two fundamental things for the reproduction of capital: goods and those who produce them (postmodernity remains imperfect: human labour is still necessary).

In this way, a parasitic system tends to produce more parasites. Eager to devour profits, the globalization of above leaves no well-being wherever it sets down its hoof. On the contrary, like the Four Horsemen of the Apocalypse, it sows, with the guarantee of an immediate harvest, hunger, misery, destruction, death.

That cycle will merely destroy the world in the simplest way: by destroying those who inhabit it. That is, of course, if others allow it....

V. Neoliberalism Correcting "Errors"

In the globalized neoliberal soap opera, the "other" is not even the villain, it is the monster whose elimination is necessary for the happy ending (that is, the "pretty woman" marries the "handsome man" and the villain redeems himself—upon proof of a sound bank account).

"Others" are a mistake in humanity. To globalize from above is to correct that error the world over. And to correct is to eliminate.

For this it is necessary to strip the "others" of the symbols that give them identity. Difference is then an error of nature. The Indians of the Americas were just that, and "civilizing" them was correcting god's work...in the name of god.

But neoliberal modernity no longer promotes the hunting of Indians or blacks. No, now it's about hunting humans...or, better yet, hunting humanity's identities. And what better human identity than culture!

If the logic of the market is that of profit (note: which is not the same as that of wealth generation), then any culture that does not respond to that logic must be eliminated. If culture is fundamentally a living mirror (even when it has death as its theme) that tells us "this I am, I was, I will be," then an attack (by commission or omission) on culture is an attack on life.

Two years ago, a Mexican journalist and writer, Vicente Leñero, on the occasion of presenting the National Science and Arts Awards, described for Mexico what could serve for the world of above:

> The governing class, the political class, the business class, not to say the ecclesiastical class, seem impervious to cultural avidity; they do not incorporate it into their own existence, perhaps because they think that the spirit of giving freely with which all works of art are conceived, that openhandedness, that generosity of the creative genius, is suspect in terms of practical utility.
>
> (Speech at the National Science and Arts Awards ceremony, in the Mexican newspaper *Reforma*, *Cultura*, Feb. 26, 2002)

Neoliberalism in the face of culture is not just a compendium of crassness and instant and "ready-made" superficialities. It is also that, but not only so. It is also a doctrine of anti-culture war, that is, of war against everything that does not respond to the logic of the market.

In addition, artists and intellectuals are suspected of thinking. And thinking is the first step to being different. If annihilating artists and intellectuals brings bad press, there is the option of starving them of oxygen. Governments professing a neoliberal creed not only do not invest in the sciences and the arts, they also snatch what little there is in the cultural sphere "to invest it in unavoidable, urgent and unpostponable priorities"…such as servicing foreign debt.

VI. Second, a Shorter, but Equally Necessary, Profile of Giraffes

Each giraffe has its own pattern of spots, and they have an excellent sense of hearing, smell and sight. Giraffes were hunted to get their thick and resilient hides, but at present they are a protected species.

VII. A World Without Giraffes?

With their ungainly gait, their obvious asymmetry, their nonchalant look, giraffes have a beautiful ugliness. Well, on further consideration, it is not that they are ugly, rather they seem very "other," with that form so far removed from the conceited, balanced symmetries that are granted to predators. The giraffe is the most emblematic image of difference in the animal world. Not only is it different, but it parades its colossal irregularity, converting its "otherness" into beauty, precisely because it is shown. Humanity too, fortunately, has its "giraffes."

There are, for example, women giraffes, persecuted and harassed not only for not striving to conform to the norms of beauty and behavior that are imposed from above ("ornaments do not think or speak, dear"), but also for brandishing their difference and struggling to be what they want to be and not what men want them to be.

There are also young giraffes, males and females, so many very reluctant to submit / people say, "to mature" / to the chain of capitulations, betrayals and prostitutions that are associated with the calendar. Youths who take to not only not hiding their asymmetry of body and soul, but who adorn it, gel it, tattoo it, attach a piercing to it, "Goth" it, "skate" it, "hip-hop" it, "punk" it, "skinhead" it, "whatever-it's-called" it, shout it out with *graffiti* on a wall, leaflet it in support of a social struggle, make it into a gesture of flipping off "the forces of order," get it studying but without profit being the driving force and objective, and make it jump when Rock, that sonorous mirror, decrees the abolition of the law of gravity and run-dude-because-here-come-the-cops-to-make-us-mature-or-who-are-going-to-bring-us-down-but-with-a-snitch-and-hurry-it-up-with-that-graffiti-that-clearly-reads-that-"the-giraffes-united-will-never-be-rugs"[3]-but-if-it-doesn't-rhyme-dude-although-if-we-are-giraffes-not-poets....

There are also the "other" giraffes: homosexual, lesbian, transsexual, transvestite and "each-according-to-their-preference" giraffes, or whatever. Not only coming out of the closet, but also flaunting their difference with a dignity that distinguishes human beings from neoliberals, sorry, from animals. No matter that they are persecuted and mocked even by those who say they want to change the world. Javier Lozano Barragán, the Catholic bishop of Zacatecas, Mexico, compared homosexuals and lesbians to cockroaches (*La Jornada*, Oct. 22, 2004, *Penultimatum*). Cockroaches are not in danger of extinction. Giraffes are. What is more, according to rigorous scientific studies, cockroaches would be the only living beings in the event of a global holocaust. It is not known whether bishops would survive.

There are also indigenous giraffes, men and women and youths, who sport their color, their language and their culture with the same gaiety and hues as their clothes, their songs, their dances, their struggles and rebellions.

And there are giraffe workers, peasants, employees, teachers, drivers, market vendors, priests, nuns, artists, intellectuals,

---

[3] Marcos is making a play here on the famous activist chant of "The people, united, will never be defeated."

undocumented [people], wearing boots or sneakers or flip-flops or *huaraches*,[4] or only with their naked feet. Giraffe people, that is.

Under neoliberalism, we other human beings, the giraffes, the ugly, the asymmetrical, that is to say, the immense majority of humanity, are hunted so as to profit from our hard skin.

There should be a law that protects us as an "endangered species." There is not. However, instead of a law, we have our resistance, our defiance, our dignity.

It is our duty to resist, because a world without giraffes would be...hmm...how shall I put it?...I know!... It would be like a *taco al pastor*,[5] but without the tortilla, meat, pineapple, cilantro, onion or salsa; that is, just the greasy food wrapper, just the food wrapper with the nostalgia of having had a taco on it that, by the way, I already scarfed down, but with the novelty that the program is just about to finish and I can't find the antacids in my backpack, and so, as the song goes, "Latin American mothers, time to give birth."[6]

I'm off. Stay tuned to the Zapatista Intergalactic Television System. I know that it's a "very" other television station, but just to let you know, a long time ago, television was black and white, and now it's in color. If we giraffes, all of us, prevail, then tomorrow life will have color, all the colors. The television?... hmm...who cares!

All right, now I'm off...

---

4 A Mexican sandal of Pre-Columbian origin.

5 Literally: "shepherd's taco," which resembles a donner kebab but is commonly made of pork.

6 I.e. Marcos is about to emit a hearty belch. The song in question here is "March of the Latin American Mothers" (1976) by Mexico's famous singer-songwriter of protest songs, José de Molina, which goes: "Latin American mothers, time to give birth/to birth more guerrilla fighters." The song became something of a "hymn" among Latin American leftists in the 1970s. Marcos' use of this refrain to refer to belching here could be taken as his mocking the macho chauvinism of the continent's old revolutionary armed Left.

On the screen (that is, on the cardboard) is now displayed:

"Here ends this special on the Recovery Channel,[7] the memory channel dedicated to giraffes and exclusively for the Zapatista Intergalactic Television System. Do not switch off, better dash off for a snack (if they are *tacos al pastor* don't be mean,[8] leave one at least. The Management)."

From the mountains of the Mexican southeast,
Subcomandante Insurgente Marcos
(Mexico, October 2004. 20 and 10)

---

[7]   Marcos is making a play on the *Discovery Channel* here.

[8]   The Spanish contains a pun here. Marcos writes, "if they are *shepherds' tacos* don't be an *ojaldras*"—the latter being both a puff/flakey pastry filled with a savory filling, but also Mexican slang for "mean."

FURTHER READING

The literature on Subcomandante Marcos in Spanish is, naturally, vast. What follow below then are works by or about the Subcomandante that are written in English.

Edited Collections of Subcomandante Marcos' Writings

Autonomedia. *¡Zapatistas! Documents of the New Mexican Revolution.* New York: Autonomedia, 1994.

Clarke, Ben, and Clifton Ross. *Voices of Fire: Communiqués and Interviews from the Zapatista Army of National Liberation.* San Francisco: Freedom Voices, 2000.

EZLN. *Critical Thought in the Face of the Capitalist Hydra.* Durham: Paperboat Press, 2016.

Ross, John, and Frank Bardacke, eds. *Shadows of a Tender Fury: The Communiqués of Subcomandante Marcos and the EZLN.* New York: Monthly Review Press, 1995.

Ruggiero, Greg, and Stewart Shahulka, eds. *Zapatista Encuentro: Documents from the 1996 Encounter For Humanity and Against Neoliberalism.* New York: Seven Stories Press, 1998.

Subcomandante Marcos. *The Story of Colors/La Historia de los Colores.* El Paso: Cinco Puntos Press, 1999.

———. *Our Word is Our Weapon.* Edited by Juana Ponce de León. New York: Seven Stories Press, 2001.

———. *Questions and Swords.* El Paso: Cinco Puntos Press, 2001.

———. *Zapatista Stories.* Translated by Dinah Livingstone. London: Katabasis, 2001.

———. *¡Ya Basta! Ten Years of the Zapatista Uprising.* Edited by Žiga Vodovnik. Oakland: AK Press, 2004.

————. *Conversations with Durito: Stories of the Zapatistas and Neoliberalism.* New York: Autonomedia, 2005.

————. *Chiapas: Resistance and Rebellion.* Coimbatore, IN: Vitiyal Pathippagam, 2005.

————. *The Other Campaign.* San Francisco: City Lights Open Media, 2006.

————. *The Speed of Dreams.* San Francisco: City Lights Open Media, 2007.

————. *Professionals of Hope: The Selected Writings of Subcomandante Marcos.* Brooklyn: The Song Cave, 2017.

————. *The Zapatistas' Dignified Rage: Final Public Speeches of Subcommander Marcos.* Edited by Nick Henck. Translated by Henry Gales. Chico: AK Press, 2018.

Interviews with Subcomandante Marcos

Benjamin, Medea. "Interview: Subcomandante Marcos." In *First World, ha ha ha!*, edited by Elaine Katzenberger, 57–70. San Francisco: City Lights Publishers, 1995.

Blixen, Samuel, and Carlos Fazio. "Interview with Marcos about Neoliberalism, the National State and Democracy." Struggle Archive. 1995. Accessed March 15, 2019. http://struggle.ws/mexico/ezln/inter_marcos_aut95.html.

de Huerta, Marta Duran, and Nicholas Higgins. "An interview with Subcomandante Insurgente Marcos, Spokesperson and Military Commander of the Zapatista National Liberation Army (EZLN)." *International Affairs* 75, no. 2 (1999): 269–279.

El Kilombo. *Beyond Resistance: Everything: An Interview with Subcomandante Insurgente Marcos.* Durham: Paperboat Press, 2007.

García Márquez, Gabriel, and Roberto Pombo. "The Punch Card and the Hour Glass: Interview with Subcomandante Marcos." *New Left Review* 9 (2001): 69–79. Accessed March 15, 2019.

http://struggle.ws/mexico/ezln/2001/marcos/gg_interview. html.

Landau, Saul. "In the Jungle with Marcos." (Interview). *The Progressive*, March 1996. Accessed March 15, 2019. https://www. thefreelibrary.com/In+the+jungle+with+Marcos.-a018049702.

McCaughan, Michael. "An Interview with Subcomandante Marcos." *NACLA Report on the Americas* 28, no. 1 (1995): 35–37. Accessed March 15, 2019. http://home.san.rr.com/ revolution/Marcos.htm.

Monsiváis, Carlos, and Hermann Bellinghausen. "Marcos Interview." Struggle Archive. January 8, 2001. Accessed March 15, 2019. http://www.struggle.ws/mexico/ezln/2001/ marcos_interview_jan.html.

Rodríguez Lascano, Sergio. "The Extra Element: Organization: An Exclusive Interview with Zapatista Subcomandante Marcos: Part I." *Rebeldía*, May 30, 2006. Accessed March 15, 2019. http://www.narconews.com/Issue41/article1856.html.

———. "A Message for the Intellectuals and their 'Magnificent Alibi to Avoid Struggle and Confrontation': An Exclusive Interview with Zapatista Subcomandante Marcos: Part II." *Rebeldía*, May 31, 2006. Accessed March 15, 2019. http:// www.narconews.com/Issue41/article1857.html.

———. "A Different Path for Latin America Rides through Mexico: An Exclusive Interview with Zapatista Subcomandante Marcos: Part III." *Rebeldía*, May 31, 2006. Accessed March 15, 2019. http://www.narconews.com/ Issue41/article1861.html.

———. "If You Listen, Mexico 2006 Seems a lot Like Chiapas in 1992: An Exclusive Interview with Zapatista Subcomandante Marcos: Part IV." *Rebeldía*, June 1, 2006. Accessed March 15, 2019. http://www.narconews.com/Issue41/article1865.html.

Simon, Joel. "The Marcos Mystery: A Chat with the Subcommander of Spin." In *The Zapatista Reader*, edited by Tom Hayden, 45–47. New York: Thunder's Mouth Press, 2002.

Subcomandante Marcos. "First Interviews with Marcos." Struggle Archive. January 1, 1994. Accessed March 15, 2019. http://www.struggle.ws/mexico/ezln/marcos_interview_jan94.html.

———. "Interview with Subcomandante Marcos." Struggle Archive. May 11, 1994. Accessed March 15, 2019. http://www.struggle.ws/mexico/ezln/marcos_interview_jan94.html.

———. "December 1994 Interview with Marcos." Struggle Archive. December 9, 1994. Accessed March 15, 2019. http://www.struggle.ws/mexico/ezln/inter_marcos_dec94.html.

———. "Interview with Marcos." Struggle Archive. August 25, 1995. Accessed March 15, 2019. http://www.struggle.ws/mexico/ezln/inter_marcos_consult_aug95.html.

———. "Never Again A Mexico Without Us." Struggle Archive. November 25, 1997. Accessed March 15, 2019. http://www.struggle.ws/mexico/ezln/1997/marcos_inter_cni_feb.html.

———. "15 Years Since the Formation of the EZLN." Struggle Archive. November 16, 1998. Accessed March 15, 2019. http://www.struggle.ws/mexico/ezln/1998/inter_marcos_nov98.html.

———. "Bellinghausen Interviews Marcos about Consulta." Struggle Archive. March 10 and 11, 1999. Accessed March 15, 2019. http://struggle.ws/mexico/ezln/1999/inter_marcos_consul_mar.html.

———. "Marcos on Peace, 3 Conditions and Globalisation." Struggle Archive. January 28, 2001. Accessed March 15, 2019. http://struggle.ws/mexico/ezln/1999/inter_marcos_consul_mar.html.

Writings on Subcomandante Marcos

A) Substantial Works

Di Piramo, Daniela. *Political Leadership in Zapatista Mexico: Marcos, Celebrity, and Charismatic Authority.* Boulder: Lynne Rienner Publishers, 2010.

————. "Beyond Modernity: Irony, Fantasy, and the Challenge to Grand Narratives in Subcomandante Marcos's Tales." *Mexican Studies/Estudios Mexicanos* 27, no. 1 (2011): 177–205.

Guillermoprieto, Alma. "Zapata's Heirs." In *Looking for History: Dispatches from Latin America.* New York: Vintage, 2002.

————. "The Unmasking." In *Looking for History: Dispatches from Latin America.* New York: Vintage, 2002.

Henck, Nick. *Subcommander Marcos: The Man and the Mask.* Durham: Duke University Press, 2007.

————. "Laying a Ghost to Rest: Subcommander Marcos' Playing of the Indigenous Card." *Estudios Mexicanos/Mexican Studies* 25, no. 1 (2009): 155–170.

————. "Subcommander Marcos and Mexico's Public Intellectuals: Octavio Rodríguez Araujo, Carlos Monsiváis, Elena Poniatowska and Pablo González Casanova." *A Contracorriente* 9, no. 1 (2011): 287–335.

————. "Subcommander Marcos' Discourse on Mexico's Intellectual Class." *Asian Journal of Latin American Studies* 25, no. 1 (2012): 35–73.

————. "The Subcommander and the Sardinian: Marcos and Gramsci." *Estudios Mexicanos/Mexican Studies* 29, no. 2 (2013): 428–458.

————. "Subcomandante Marcos: The Latest Reader." *The Latin Americanist* 58, no. 2 (2014): 49–73.

————. "Adiós Marcos: A Fond Farewell to the Subcommander Who Simply Ceased to Exist." *A Contracorriente* 12, no. 2 (2015): 401–421.

_____. *Insurgent Marcos: The Political-Philosophical Formation of the Zapatista Subcommander*. Raleigh, NC: Editorial A Contracorriente, 2016.

_____. Introduction to *The Zapatistas' Dignified Rage: Final Public Speeches of Subcommander Marcos*, 7–33. Chico: AK Press, 2018.

Herlinghaus, Hermann. "Subcomandante Marcos: Narrative Policy and Epistemological Project." *Journal of Latin American Cultural Studies* 14, no. 1 (2005): 53–74.

Higgins, Nicholas P. "Visible Indians: Subcomandante Marcos and the 'Indianization' of the Zapatista Army of National Liberation." In *Understanding the Chiapas Rebellion: Modernist Visions and the Invisible Indian*. Austin: University of Texas Press, 2004.

Jörgensen, Beth. "Making History: Subcomandante Marcos in the Mexican Chronicle." In *Documents in Crisis: Nonfiction Literatures in Twentieth-Century Mexico*. New York: SUNY Press, 2011.

Krauze, Enrique. "Subcomandante Marcos: The Rise and Fall of a Guerrillero." In *Redeemers: Ideas and Power in Latin America*. New York: Harper Perennial, 2011.

Martín, Desirée A. "'Todos Somos Santos,' Subcomandante Marcos and the EZLN." In *Borderland Saints: Secular Sanctity in Chicano/a and Mexican Culture*. London: Rutgers University Press, 2014.

Mato, Shigeko. "Subcomandante Marcos' Performance: Intellectual Consciousness and Appropriation." In *Co-optation, Complicity, and Representation: Desire and Limits for Intellectuals in Twentieth-Century Mexican Fiction*. New York: Peter Lang Inc., 2010.

Meisenhalter, Fernando. *A Biography of the Subcomandante Marcos: Rebel Leader of the Zapatistas in Mexico*. Kindle, 2017.

Oppenheimer, Andrés. "Marcos" and "Unmasking Marcos." In *Bordering on Chaos*. Boston: Back Bay Books, 1998.

Weinberg, Bill. "Behind the Lines with Marcos." In *Homage to Chiapas*. London: Verso, 2000.

B) Shorter Pieces

Bardach, Ann Louise. "Mexico's Poet Rebel." *Vanity Fair*, July 1994, 68–74 and 130–135.

Bob, Clifford. "The Making of an Anti-Globalization Icon: Mexico's Zapatista Uprising." In *The Marketing of Rebellion*. New York: Cambridge University Press, 2005.

Gogol, Eugene. "Mexico's Revolutionary Forms of Organization: The Zapatistas and the Indigenous Autonomous Communities in Resistance." In *Utopia and the Dialectic in Latin American Liberation*. Leiden: Brill, 2016.

———. "The Zapatistas and the Dialectic." In *Utopia and the Dialectic in Latin American Liberation*. Leiden: Brill, 2016.

Graebner, Cornelia. "Subcomandante Insurgente Marcos." *The Literary Encyclopedia*. 2011. http://www.litencyc.com/.

Henck, Nick. "Subcomandante Marcos." In *Iconic Mexico: An Encyclopedia from Acapulco to Zócalo*, edited by Eric Zolov, 556–562. Santa Barbara: ABC-CLIO, 2015.

Klein, Naomi. "The Unknown Icon." In *The Zapatista Reader*, edited by Tom Hayden, 114–123. New York: Thunder's Mouth Press, 2002.

Monsiváis, Carlos. "From the Subsoil to the Mask that Reveals." In *The Zapatista Reader*, edited by Tom Hayden, 123–132. New York: Thunder's Mouth Press, 2002.

Montalbán, Manuel Vázquez. "Marcos: Mestizo Culture on the Move." In *The Zapatista Reader*, edited by Tom Hayden, 472–483. New York: Thunder's Mouth Press, 2002.

Poniatowska, Elena. "Voices from the Jungle: Subcommander Marcos and Culture." In *The Zapatista Reader*, edited by Tom Hayden, 73–81. New York: Thunder's Mouth Press, 2002.

Stavans, Ilan. "Unmasking Marcos." In *The Zapatista Reader*, edited by Tom Hayden, 386–395. New York: Thunder's Mouth Press, 2002.

Steele, Cynthia. "The Rainforest Chronicle of Subcomandante Marcos." In *The Contemporary Mexican Chronicle*, edited by

Ignacio Corona and Beth E. Jörgensen, 245–255. New York: SUNY Press, 2002.

Tormey, Simon. *"Ya Basta!:* A Brief Excursus on Marcos and 'Zapatismo.'" In *Anti-Capitalism: A Beginners Guide.* Oxford: Oneworld Publications, 2004.

Vanden Berghe, Kristine, and Bart Maddens. "Ethnocentrism, Nationalism and Post-nationalism in the Tales of Subcomandante Marcos." *Mexican Studies/Estudios Mexicanos* 20, no. 1 (2004): 123–144.

Books on the Zapatista Movement in General

Conant, Jeff. *A Poetics of Resistance: The Revolutionary Public Relations of the Zapatista Insurgency.* Oakland: AK Press, 2010.

Hayden, Tom. *The Zapatista Reader.* New York: Thunder's Mouth Press, 2002.

Holloway, John, and Eloína Peláez, eds. *Zapatista! Reinventing Revolution in Mexico.* London: Pluto Press, 1998.

Khasnabish, Alex. *Zapatistas: Rebellion from the Grassroots to the Global.* London: Zed Books, 2010.

Mentinis, Mihalis. *Zapatistas: The Chiapas Revolt and what it means for Radical Politics.* London: Pluto Press, 2006.

Muñoz Ramírez, Gloria. *The Fire and the Word.* San Francisco: City Lights Publishers, 2008.

Ross, John. *Rebellion from the Roots: Indian Uprising in Chiapas.* Monroe, ME: Common Courage Press, 1995.

———. *The War Against Oblivion: The Zapatista Chronicles 1994–2000.* Monroe, ME: Common Courage Press, 2000.

———. *¡Zapatistas! Making Another World Possible: Chronicles of Resistance 2000–2006.* New York: Nation Books, 2006.

Audio-Visual and Online Sources

Documentaries

Miranda, Guadalupe and Maria I. Roque. La Companeras Tienen Grado = Zapatista Women. Mexico: Centro de Capacitacion Cinemafotografica, 1996.

Calonico, Cristian. Marcos: Historia y Palabra = Marcos: Word and History. Mexico City: Producciones Marca Diablo, 1996.

Eichert, Benjamin, Rick Rowley and Stale Sandberg. Zapatista. New York, NY: Big Noise Films, 1998.

Wild, Nettie. *A Place Called Chiapas: A Film.* New York, N.Y.: Zeitgeist Films, 1998.

Colombo, Santiago. *Storm from the Mountain: Zapatistas Take Mexico City.* New York, N.Y.: Big Noise Films, 2001.

Nava, Francesca. *The Other Mexico.* Los Angeles, CA: Choices, Inc, 2008.

Websites

The following contain translations into English of many of Marcos', and the Zapatistas', communiqués, declarations, interviews, and other important documents:

Enlace Zapatista: http://enlacezapatista.ezln.org.mx/

Irish Mexico Group: http://www.struggle.ws/mexico/ezlnco.html

El Kilombo Intergaláctico: http://www.elkilombo.org/ezln/

Europa Zapatista: www.europazapatista.org/?tags=pl-en

Ours Reemerging Translations: galestranslations.blogspot.com

NOTES

1   I use "alter-globalisation" as opposed to "anti-globalisation" since
     Marcos and the Zapatistas (and many others besides) are not
     technically against globalisation as such (meaning the increasing
     interconnectedness of people all over the globe), but rather are
     opposed to specifically neoliberal capitalist globalisation.

2   On Marcos' iconic status, see Nick Henck, "Subcomandante
     Marcos," in *Iconic Mexico: An Encyclopedia from Acapulco to
     Zócalo*, ed. Eric Zolov (California: ABC-CLIO, 2015), 556–
     562; Naomi Klein, "The Unknown Icon," in *The Zapatista
     Reader*, ed. Tom Hayden (New York: Thunder's Mouth Press,
     2002), 114–123; and Clifford Bob, "The Making of an Anti-
     Globalization Icon: Mexico's Zapatista Uprising," in his *The
     Marketing of Rebellion* (New York: Cambridge University Press,
     2005), 117–177, esp. at 161–164. For Marcos as a multicultural
     hero and contemporary legend, see José Alejos García, "Ethnic
     identity and the Zapatistas Rebellion in Chiapas," in *National
     Identities and Sociopolítical Changes in Latin America*, eds. M.
     Durán–Cogan and A. Gómez Moriana (New York: Routledge,
     2001), 160–177. Finally, Immanuel Wallerstein, in his "Marcos,
     Mandela, and Gandhi," *Commentary* No. 59, March 1, 2001,
     http://www.binghamton.edu/fbc/archive/59en.htm,   likens
     the Subcomandante to Gandhi and Mandela, while Gary H.
     Gossen, "Who is the Comandante of Subcomandante Marcos?,"
     in *Indigenous Revolts in Chiapas and the Andean Highlands*, eds.
     Kevin Gosner and Arij Ouweneel (Amsterdam: CEDLA, 1996),
     107–120, makes the comparison with Kennedy.

3   See Bertrand de la Grange and Maite Rico, *Subcomandante
     Marcos: la genial impostura* (Mexico City: El País Aguilar, 1998),
     70. Rafael's father recalls that "before the age of five, without

having even learned to read, he already knew how to recite." He cites the example of Marcos Rafael Blanco Belmonte's 495-word poem "The Sower," which Rafael could recite from memory. See Ann Louise Bardach, "Mexico's Poet Rebel," *Vanity Fair* 57, July 1994, 67–68, where Marcos recalls: "I learned to read in my house, not at school; so when I went to school I had a great advantage, because I was already well read."

4   Bardach, "Mexico's Poet Rebel," 67.

5   See Autonomedia, *¡Zapatistas! Documents of the New Mexican Revolution* (New York: Autonomedia, 1994), 197.

6   In de la Grange and Rico, *Subcomandante Marcos*, 75.

7   In FLN, *Estatutos de las Fuerzas de Liberación Nacional* (Mexico City, Aug. 6, 1980); translated into English as *Statutes of the Forces of National Liberation* (Montreal: Abraham Guillen Press & Arm The Spirit, 2003), 5.

8   For the importance of Guevara to Rafael/Marcos, see Nick Henck, *Subcommander Marcos: The Man and the Mask* (Durham: Duke University Press, 2007), 21, 27–28, 52, 75, 82, 154, 165, 288–290, and 365–366; Nick Henck, "Subcomandante Marcos: The Latest Reader," *The Latin Americanist*, 58, no. 2 (2014): 49–73; and Nick Henck *Insurgent Marcos: The Political-Philosophical Formation of the Zapatista Subcommander* (Raleigh: Editorial A Contracorriente, 2016), 52–55.

9   In Yvon Le Bot, *El sueño zapatista* (Mexico City: Editorial Anagrama, 1997), 124 (my translation).

10 On the non-dogmatic, ideologically heterodox nature of the FLN, see Nick Henck, *Insurgent Marcos*, 49–51.

11 Nick Henck, *Subcommander Marcos*, 57–64, provides a more detailed account of the abject living conditions and appalling abuses endured by Chiapas' indigenous peasantry.

12 Nick Henck, *Subcommander Marcos*, 114, quotes Marcos as saying: "We Zapatistas passed from tens to thousands in a short time; I am speaking of a single year, 1988–9. We passed from being eighty combatants to 1,300 in less than a year," and as

stating that around this time there took place "a massive growth of the EZLN."

[13] See Marcos' statement to this effect in Subcomandante Marcos, *The Zapatistas' Dignified Rage: Final Public Speeches of Subcommander Marcos* (Chico: AK Press, 2018), 116:

> But in the case of an indigenous people, the death of their children means their disappearance as a people.... The mortality of indigenous people, of indigenous children, intensified the problem.... The dilemma was very simple: if we rise up in arms, they are going to defeat us, but it is going to draw attention and going to improve conditions for the indigenous. If we do not rise up in arms, we are going to survive, but we are going to disappear as Indian peoples.

[14] See Nick Henck, *Subcommander Marcos*, 189, where Marcos is quoted as describing the uprising as "only a call of attention" and as stating: "we didn't go to war on 1 January to kill or to be killed. We went to war to make ourselves heard."

[15] I.e. when the Zapatistas declared war on the Mexican government and rose up in arms.

[16] In Subcomandante Marcos, *The Zapatistas' Dignified Rage*, 137.

[17] In Subcomandante Marcos, *The Zapatistas' Dignified Rage*, 218.

[18] *EZLN: Documentos y Comunicados* Volumes 1–5 (Mexico City, 1994, 1995, 1997, 2000 and 2003).

[19] With Sergio Rodríguez Lascano (May 2006), Jesús Quintero (June 2006), the El Kilombo Collective (January 2007), Reymundo Reynoso (January 2007), and Laura Castellanos (November 2007).

[20] Tim Padgett, "The Return of Guerrilla Chic," *Newsweek*, May 1996, 14.

[21] In Gabriel García Márquez and Roberto Pombo, "The Punch Card and the Hour Glass: Interview with Subcomandante Marcos," *New Left Review* 9 (2001), 74.

22 In their *The Sixth Declaration of the Lacandon Jungle*, almost certainly formulated by Marcos (http://sixthdeclaration. blogspot.jp/2013/06/full-text.html).

23 Reproduced and translated in John Ross' and Frank Bardacke's, eds., *Shadows of a Tender Fury: The Communiqués of Subcomandante Marcos and the EZLN* (New York: Monthly Review Press, 1995), 251.

24 Idem.

25 See above, p. 24. For more on this farewell speech, including a translation of it, see Subcomandante Marcos, *The Zapatistas' Dignified Rage*, 211ff.

26 A translation of this can be found on the Enlace Zapatista website, at: https://bit.ly/2pc50DR.

27 For more on these presentations, and translations of them, see Subcomandante Marcos, *The Zapatistas' Dignified Rage*, 41–108.

28 Again, for more on these presentations, and translations of them, see Subcomandante Marcos, *The Zapatistas' Dignified Rage*, 133–207.

29 For a translation of all the speeches made by the Zapatistas at this symposium, including those of Subcomandantes Galeano and Moisés, see EZLN, *Critical Thought in the Face of the Capitalist Hydra Vol. I* (Durham: Paperboat Press, 2016).

30 Translations of these can be found on the Enlace Zapatista website (http://enlacezapatista.ezln.org.mx) listed according to date.

31 Translations of these can be found on the Enlace Zapatista website, at: https://bit.ly/2oO7o2T and https://bit.ly/2TcAYgC.

32 Translations of Galeano's announcement of the forthcoming event and its program can be found online (respectively): https://bit.ly/2CoM4cP; and https://bit.ly/2Havf6N.

33 In Robert M. Carmack, Janine L. Gasco and Gary H. Gossen, eds., *The Legacy of Mesoamerica: History and Culture of a Native American Civilization (Second Edition)* (Oxford: Routledge, 2007), 391. He continues "This constitutes a formal recognition of what Indians have long understood, that he truly speaks on their behalf and that his charismatic leadership carries their blessings and moral authority."

34 The "March" was in actuality a convoy of 38 coaches, accompanied by 120 vehicles bearing supporters. It aimed at drawing attention not only to the Zapatistas themselves but also to the inauguration that month of the civilian solidarity organization, the Zapatista Front for National Liberation (FZLN in Spanish), that they had called upon civil society to establish.

35 A *mestizo* is a person of mixed European-Amerindian heritage and/or descent.

36 In his "A Guerrilla with a Difference," in *The Zapatista Reader*, ed. Tom Hayden, (New York: Thunder's Mouth Press, 2002), 350.

37 In Marcos' interview with Julio Scherer García, "La entrevista insólita," *Proceso*. No. 1271, March 2001, 13 (my translation).

38 Enrique Krauze, *Redeemers: Ideas and Power in Latin America* (New York: Harper Perennial, 2011), 448.

39 The quotations are from an interview Marcos granted Elena Poniatowska on July 24, 1994 (https://bit.ly/2HmbkEI). Poniatowska asks why the Subcomandante is so enamoured with public intellectuals and he responds: "because they are opinion leaders…[and] influence public opinion and civil society" (my translation).

40 Respectively, in: Nick Henck, *Subcommander Marcos*, 271; and Subcomandante Marcos, *¡Ya Basta! Ten Years of the Zapatista Uprising*, ed. Žiga Vodovnik (Oakland: AK Press, 2004), 139.

41 In Laura Castellanos, *Corte de Caja: Entrevista al Subcomandante Marcos* (Mexico City: Grupo Editorial Endira Mexico, 2008), 92 (my translation).

42 John Ross, *The War Against Oblivion: The Zapatista Chronicles 1994–2000* (Monroe, Maine: Common Courage Press, 2000), 53; and Bill Weinberg, *Homage to Chiapas* (London: Verso, 2000), 119.

43 See Marcos, "Putting Out the Fire with Gasoline (Postscript to the Cartoon)," Enlace Zapatista, January 11, 2013, https://bit.ly/2HvkNtJ, where he points out that an August 15, 2012 denunciation by the Zapatista Good Government Committee

of La Realidad was posted on the Zapatistas' homepage for 24 days and garnered 1080 hits, whereas a cartoon he posted on the same webpage received more than 5,000 viewings in less than 48 hours.

[44] The cult of the rebel is especially powerful in Mexico: many of its national heroes are insurgents and revolutionaries such as Hidalgo, Morelos, Guerrero, Zapata, and Villa—a rebel tradition to which Marcos has laid claim.

[45] Alma Guillermoprieto, *Looking for History: Dispatches from Latin America* (New York: Vintage, 2002), 216.

[46] By, respectively, Régis Debray, "*A demain, Zapata!*", *Le Monde*, March 17, 1995; Juan Pellicer, "La gravedad y la gracia: el discurso del Subcomandante Marcos," *Revista Iberoamericana* 62, no. 174 (1996), 199; Ilan Stavans, *The Oxford Book of Latin American Essays* (Oxford: Oxford University Press, 1997), 481; and Julia Preston and Samuel Dillon, *Opening Mexico: The Making of a Democracy* (New York: Farrar, 2004), 449.

[47] In his *A Poetics of Resistance: The Revolutionary Public Relations of the Zapatista Insurgency* (Oakland: AK Press, 2010), 358, n. 55.

[48] In Laura Castellanos, *Corte de Caja*, 105 (my translation).

[49] Ibid, 105.

[50] To list solely those who have written in English about the influence of *Don Quixote* on Marcos, there is: Luis Correa–Díaz, "Cervantes in America: Between New World Chronicle and Chivalric Romance," in *A Twice-Told Tale: Re-Inventing the Encounter in Iberian/Iberian American Literature and Film*, eds. Santiago Juan-Navarro and Theodore Robert Young (Newark: University of Delaware Press, 2001); Valeria Wagner and Alejandro Moreira, "Toward a Quixotic Pragmatism: The Case of the Zapatista Insurgence," *Boundary 2* 30, no. 3 (2003), 200f; Kristine Vanden Berghe, "The Quixote in the Stories of Subcomandante Marcos," in *The International Don Quixote*, eds. Theo D'haen and Reindert Dhondt (Amsterdam: Brill Rodopi, 2009), 53–69; and Jeff Conant, *A Poetics of Resistance*, (Chico: AK Press, 2010), 63ff, 170ff, 211–212, and 223–225.

51 Concerning the influence of the poems of León Felipe and Miguel Hernández on the Subcomandante, see Juan Pellicer, "La gravedad y la gracia," 200, 206, and 208, and also his "El subcomandante Marcos: posdata de las armas y las letras," *Universitas Humanistica* 51/XXIX (2001), 117 and 123–124; while Kristine Vanden Berghe, *Narrativa de la rebelión zapatista: los relatos del Subcomandante Marcos* (Madrid: Iberoamericana Editorial Vervuert, 2005), 174–180, draws attention to Frederico García Lorca's impact on Marcos' writing.

52 These quotations are from Enrique Krauze, *Redeemers*, 441; Jorge Volpi, *La guerra y las palabras* (Barcelona: Editorial Seix Barral, 2004), 300; and Luis Hernández Navarro, *Sentido contrario* (Mexico City: IRD Éditions, 2007), 100, respectively.

53 For more details of the Army's find of more than 70 books, see Nick Henck, "Subcomandante Marcos: The Latest Reader," 62; or Nick Henck, *Insurgent Marcos*, 36–37.

54 See Marcos' interview with Juan Gelman, "'Nada que ver con las armas,' Entrevista exclusiva con el Subcomandante Marcos," (1996). An example of one of Marcos' political poems from around this period can be found translated in Nicholas P. Higgins, *Understanding the Chiapas Rebellion: Modernist Visions and the Invisible Indian* (Austin: University of Texas Press, 2004), 159ff.

55 Marcos, "Por Radio UNAM, 18 de marzo," *Chiapas: la palabra de los armados de verdad y fuego Vol II*, (Mexico City: Editorial Fuenteovejuna, 1995), 72 (my translation).

56 Ibid., 82 (my translation).

57 In "Entrevista con el Subcomandante Marcos, por Raymundo Reynoso," CEDOZ, January 9, 2007, http://www.cedoz.org/site/content.php?doc=518&cat=16 (my translation).

58 In Laura Castellanos, *Corte de Caja*, 96 (my translation).

59 In Gabriel García Márquez and Roberto Pombo, "The Punch Card and the Hour Glass: Interview with Subcomandante Marcos," 77–78.

60 Notably absent from the Subcomandante's communiqués are references to such philosophers and political theorists as

Adorno, Althusser, Badiou, Balibar, Baudrillard, Chomsky, Deleuze, Derrida, Fanon, Gramsci, Guattari, Habermas, Hardt, Heidegger, Horkheimer, Lacan, Laclau, Lévi–Strauss, Mao, Marcuse, Mouffe, Negri, Pêcheux, Poulantzas, and Trotsky.

61 In her "Antonio Gramsci and the Palabra Verdadera: The Political Discourse of Mexico's Guerrilla Forces," *Journal of Interamerican Studies and World Affairs* 41, no. 2 (1999), 42.

62 In Subcomandante Marcos, *Conversations with Durito: Stories of the Zapatistas and Neoliberalism* (New York: Autonomedia, 2005), 110.

63 From a conversation with Spanish crime novelist, poet, and essayist Manuel Vázquez Montalbán, which Marcos relates in a letter. Accessible at http://www.jornada.unam.mx/2004/11/29/06an1cul.php (my translation).

64 In Gabriel García Márquez and Roberto Pombo, "Punch Card," 77 and 78.

65 The novel was written and published in instalments with the authors taking turns to write a chapter, each taking up where the other had left off.

66 In, respectively, her essay entitled "Can a Cook Explode Like a Bomb?," in Subcomandante Marcos, *Questions and Swords: Folktales of the Zapatista Revolution* (El Paso: Cinco Puntos Press, 2001), 107; and her "Voices from the Jungle: Subcomandante Marcos and Culture," in *The Zapatista Reader*, 377.

67 "Detrás de nosotros estamos ustedes: la ironía en el discurso del subcomandante Marcos," *Signos Literarios y Lingüísticos* 4, no. 2 (2002), 104–106, retrieved from https://bit.ly/2JhnmAY.

68 In his introduction to *Saisons de la Digne Rage* (Paris: Climats Éditions, 2009), 8.

69 *Understanding the Chiapas Rebellion*, 156–157.

70 "Zapatismo Urbano," (in "Zapatismo as Political and Cultural Practice," ed. Manuel Callahan), *Humboldt Journal of Social Relations Special Issue* 29, no. 1 (2005), 175–176.

71 In, respectively, her *Political Leadership in Zapatista Mexico: Marcos, Celebrity, and Charismatic Authority* (Boulder: Lynne

Rienner Publishers, 2010), 124–125; and his *Saisons de la Digne Rage*, 34 and 36.

72 E.g. Lorenzo Meyer, "Turbio lenguaje del poder," *Excélsior*, March 17, 1994: 1, 10, and 36, retrieved from https://bit. ly/2Jh8J0H; Gustavo Esteva, *Celebration of Zapatismo* (New Delhi: Daanish Books, 2012). *Dissenting Knowledges Pamphlet Series*, no. 1 (Penang, Malaysia, 2004), 138; Luis Hernández Navarro, *Sentido contrario*, 103; Daniela Di Piramo, *Political Leadership in Zapatista Mexico*, 124–125; and Cornelia Graebner, "Subcomandante Insurgente Marcos," in *The Literary Encyclopedia*, (2011), 2, http:// www.litencyc.com/.

73 Jorge Volpi, "La novela del alzamiento Zapatista," El Pais, Opinion, December 28, 2003, https://bit.ly/2UJxAM4 (my translation); and Luis Hernández Navarro, *Sentido contrario*, 104 (my translation).

74 In his "Turbio lenguaje del poder," 10 and 36 (my translation).

75 In Yvon Le Bot, *El sueño zapatista*, 349–350 (my translation).

76 Nick Henck, *Insurgent Marcos*, 169, collects Marcos' references to the Zapatistas' words being weapons.

77 In his *Lenin and Philosophy and Other Essays*, trans. Ben Brewster (New York: Monthly Review Press, 2001), 21–22. Again, see Nick Henck, *Insurgent Marcos*, 75–127, for a detailed discussion of how Althusser's works, including this one, influenced considerably Rafael Guillén, the student who would become the Subcomandante.

78 In his "La novela del alzamiento Zapatista" (my translation).

79 Marcos, in Juan Gelman, "Nada que ver con las armas," states that the culture clash that arose from contact with indigenous communities was "noteworthy" in terms of the resultant "use of language in relation to the political…" (my translation).

80 On Marcos being a pamphleteer, see Enrique Krauze, *Redeemers*, 441, and Christopher Domínguez Michael, "El prosista armado," *Letras Libres*, January 1999, https://bit.ly/2Fgv36L (my translation).

81 References to a "new Mexico" appear in writings dated December 31, 1993; January 20, 1994; and June 10, 1994. For

these quotations, translated and in context, see Autonomedia, *¡Zapatistas! Documents of the New Mexican Revolution*, 52, 116 and 333, respectively.

82 In, respectively, Bertha Rodríguez Santos, "At the Zócalo, May 1st, Marcos Warns the Rich: 'We're Taking Everything!': The Other Campaign Arrives at the U.S. Embassy, Adding Itself to the Boycott in Support of Mexican Migrants," *Narco News*, May 8, 2006, https://bit.ly/2uaX5tO; and his speech to students in Mexico City on May 2, 2006, https://bit.ly/2TJDjos (my translation).

83 In a communiqué entitled "Sounds of Silence and the July '97 elections," (July 1, 1997), http://struggle.ws/mexico/ezln/ezln_election_1jul97.html.

84 Quoted and translated in Xochitl Leyva Solano, "Geopolitics of Knowledge and the Neo-Zapatista Social Movement Networks," in *The Movements of Movements. Part I: What Makes Us Move?*, ed. Jai Sen (Oakland: PM Press, 2017), 170.

85 For example, in a communiqué entitled "The table at San Andrés" (March 1998), in Subcomandante Marcos, *¡Ya Basta!*, 290.

86 In Subcomandante Marcos, *The Speed of Dreams* (San Francisco: City Lights Publishers, 2007), 282, 284, and 285.

87 In Elaine Katzenberger ed., *First World, ha ha ha!* (New York: City Lights Publishers, 1995), 109–110. For an impassioned portrayal of women's participation in the EZLN, see Commander Hortensia's speech, entitled "Fifth Wind: A Dignified and Feminine Rage" at the Festival of Dignified Rage (January 4, 2009), in Subcomandante Marcos, *The Zapatistas' Dignified Rage*, 177ff.

88 See, for example, Marcos' August 2004 communiqué entitled "Reading a Video, Part Two: Two Flaws," https://bit.ly/2ucAzkd; and his January 2009 speech "Sixth Wind: An Other Dignified Rage" in Subcomandante Marcos, *The Zapatistas' Dignified Rage*, 181ff.

89 In Yvon Le Bot, *El sueño zapatista*, 347–348 (my translation).

[90] In their *Basta!: Land and Rebellion in Chiapas* (Oakland: Food First Books, 1999), 158.

[91] In Claire Brewster, *Responding to Crisis in Contemporary Mexico: The Political Writings of Paz, Fuentes, Monsiváis, and Poniatowska* (Tucson: University of Arizona Press, 2005), 150.

[92] In David Thelen, "Mexico's Cultural Landscapes: A Conversation with Carlos Monsiváis," *The Journal of American History* 86, no. 2 (1999), 613–614.

[93] In Tom Hayden ed., *The Zapatista Reader*, 216.

[94] In, respectively, Subcomandante Marcos, *¡Ya Basta!*, 61, and Subcomandante Marcos, *Conversations with Durito*, 119.

[95] Subcomandante Marcos, *Our Word is Our Weapon*, ed. Juana Ponce de León (New York: Seven Stories Press, 2002), 167; here I have slightly modified the translation.

[96] In Subcomandante Marcos, *Dignified Rage*, 239.

[97] In Autonomedia, *¡Zapatistas!*, 116. See also Marcos' blistering attack on Mexican modernity in his communiqué entitled "Above and Below: Masks and Silences," in Subcomandante Marcos, *¡Ya Basta!*, 319–341, esp. 321ff (dated July 1998).

[98] In their *Basta!*, 155.

[99] In Le Bot, *El sueño zapatista*, 212 and 298 respectively (my translation).

[100] In Marcos, *Conversations with Durito*, 54.

[101] For example: "The Story of Durito and Neoliberalism" (April 1994); "Durito II: Neoliberalism Seen From La Lacandona" (March 1995); "Durito III: The Story of Neoliberalism and the Labor Movement" (April 1995); "Durito IV: Neoliberalism and the Party-State System" (June 1995); "Durito VI: Neoliberalism, Chaotic Theory of Economic Chaos" (July 1995); and "Durito IX: Neoliberalism, History as a Tale...Badly Told" (April 1996). These are collected in Subcomandante Marcos, *Conversations with Durito*.

[102] In Subcomandante Marcos, *¡Ya Basta!*, 155.

[103] In Subcomandante Marcos, *¡Ya Basta!*, 184–185.

[104] In Subcomandante Marcos, *¡Ya Basta!*, 321 and 325. NB The translator renders "Estado de Derecho" literally but awkwardly

"State of Law"; I have preferred to substitute it here with the more natural "Rule of Law."

[105] In EZLN, *Documentos y comunicados 3* (Mexico City: Ediciones Era, 1997), 287 (my translation).

[106] In their *Living at the Edges of Capitalism: Adventures in Exile and Mutual Aid* (Oakland: University of California Press, 2016), 148.

[107] In a communiqué entitled "Sobre el próximo proceso electoral" (June 19, 2000), quoted and translated in Richard Stahler-Sholk, "Globalization and Social Movement Resistance: The Zapatista Rebellion in Chiapas, Mexico," *New Political Science* 23, no. 4 (2001), 497. For a full version of this communiqué and an alternative translation, see http://www.narconews. com/Issue41/marcos1.html. See too, Marcos' communiqué entitled "Sounds of Silence and the July '97 elections" (July 1, 1997) that states, "Democracy is not solely electoral, but it is also electoral. The electoral arena does not just refer to the confrontation of candidates and/or political proposals at the ballot box…"; posted at: http://struggle.ws/mexico/ezln/ezln_election_1jul97.html. Similarly, see also Marcos in Yvon Le Bot, *El sueño zapatista*, 281.

[108] In Yvon Le Bot, *sueño zapatista*, 281–283 (my translation).

[109] In his interview with Marta Duran de Huerta and Nicholas Higgins, "An Interview with Subcomandante Insurgente Marcos, Spokesperson and Military Commander of the Zapatista National Liberation Army (EZLN)," *International Affairs* 75, no. 2 (1999), 271–272.

[110] Ibid., 271–272.

[111] In his "Of Zapatismo: Reflections on the Folkloric and the Impossible in a Subaltern Insurrection," in *The Politics of Culture in the Shadow of Capital*, eds. Lisa Lowe and David Lloyd (Durham: Duke University Press, 1997), 411.

[112] In his "El nudo de Chiapas," in *Chiapas: el alzamiento*, (Mexico City: La Jornada Ediciones, 1994), 109.

[113] In David Thelen, "Mexico's Cultural Landscapes," 613.

114 "Interview with Medea Benjamin," *First World*, 58.

115 In her "Subcomandante Insurgente Marcos," *The Literary Encyclopedia* (2011), 4; accessible at: http://www.litencyc.com/.

116 Díaz-Polanco is quoted and translated in Shannan L. Mattiace, *To See with Two Eyes* (Albuquerque: University of New Mexico Press, 2003), 168, n. 2; these statements by Mattiace herself can be found in the same book, on pages 21 and 89 (respectively).

117 Technically speaking of course, women constitute a numerical majority in most countries but they commonly experience the kind of unequal or discriminatory treatment associated with minorities.

118 In Autonomedia, *¡Zapatistas!*, 283.

119 In Subcomandante Marcos, *The Zapatistas' Dignified Rage*, 181.

120 In Subcomandante Marcos, *The Speed of Dreams*, 276.

121 This presentation can be found in Subcomandante Marcos, *The Speed of Dreams*, 330–336.

122 This story can be found translated online at: https://bit.ly/2m9PidZ.

123 For this story, and the two anecdotes that follow, see Subcomandante Marcos, *The Zapatistas' Dignified Rage*, 154ff, 186ff, and 184ff, respectively.

124 This presentation, entitled "The Vision of the Vanquished," can be found translated in EZLN, *Critical Thought*, 106–114.

125 Posted online at: http://struggle.ws/mexico/ezln/1999/marcos_pride_june.html.

126 In Gabriel García Márquez and Roberto Pombo, "The Punch Card and the Hour Glass: Interview with Subcomandante Marcos," 71.

127 In her "The Rainforest Chronicle of Subcomandante Marcos," in *The Contemporary Mexican Chronicle*, eds. Ignacio Corona and Beth E. Jörgensen (New York: SUNY Press, 2002), 245–255, esp. 248.

128 In Marcos, *The Speed of Dreams*, 276–277.

129 Mark Swier, "'Other Loves' in the 'Other Campaign': Oaxaca's Queer Community Looks for Common Ground with the Latest Phase of Zapatista Struggle," *The Narco News Bulletin*, March 24, 2006, http://narconews.com/Issue40/article1691.html.

130   In Subcomandante Marcos, *Our Word*, 440.

131   Marcos in Autonomedia, *¡Zapatistas!*, 298.

132   In a communiqué entitled "Sounds of Silence and the July '97 elections."

133   In, respectively, "The View from La Realidad," *The New Republic*, August 2001, 32–33; and "La novela del alzamiento Zapatista," *El País*, Opinión, December 28, 2003, https://bit. ly/2UJxAM4 (my translation).

134   In *Zapatistas: Rebellion from the Grassroots to the Global* (London: Zed Books, 2010), 71.

135   Mexican public intellectuals Octavio Paz, Carlos Fuentes and Enrique Krauze have all expressed admiration for Marcos. (For quotations by Paz and Fuentes, see Régis Debray, "A Guerrilla With a Difference," *The Zapatista Reader*, 348; for Krauze, see his *Mexico: Biography of Power* (New York: Harper Perennial, 1997), 793.)

136   In her "Voices from the Jungle: Subcomandante Marcos and Culture," *The Zapatista Reader*, 378.

137   Stavans states, "no career is more discredited in Mexico than that of a politician," in *The Zapatista Reader*, 395. Similarly, Mexican journalist Luis Hernández Navarro has stated, "The Mexican political class is about to exhaust its last reserves of credibility…" in his "Images of the Dirty TV-War: The Hour of Mediacracy," *Latin American Perspectives* 147, vol. 33, no. 2 (2006), 73; while Mexican scholar and activist Fernanda Navarro writes: "[I]n my country…all politicians…have shown the great degradation of the governing class, acting with an incredible corruption, impunity, and violence," in her "Vive la Crise!," in *The Concept in Crisis: Reading Capital Today*, ed. Nick Nesbitt, (Durham: Duke University Press, 2017), 290–291.

138   Lorenzo Meyer, "Turbio lenguaje del poder," *Excélsior*, March 17, 1994, 36, accessible at: https://bit.ly/2Y4INIU.

139   For example, Marcos made statements regarding a "new Mexico" on December 31, 1993; January 20, 1994; and June 10, 1994. He referred to a "new world" on February 2, 1994; February 14,

1994; March 1, 1994; and March 5, 1994. (For these quotations, translated and in context, see Autonomedia, *¡Zapatistas!*, respectively 52, 116, and 333; and 129, 188, 246, and 254.)

140   Quoted and translated Autonomedia, *¡Zapatistas!*, 246.

141   In Subcomandante Marcos, ¡*Ya Basta!*, 200.

142   The Spanish original is posted online at: https://bit. ly/2O9518c. The translation here is from Luis Hernández Navarro, "Zapatismo Today and Tomorrow," (January 16, 2004) Americas Program, Interhemispheric Resource Center (IRC); posted online at: https://bit.ly/2JiLMdB.

143   In Subcomandante Marcos, *Our Word*, 186.

144   In Subcomandante Marcos, *Our Word*, 194.

145   The communiqué is dated September 18, 2008, and has been translated and posted online at: https://bit.ly/2FbN6JO.

146   Naomi Klein, in her "The Unknown Icon," *The Zapatista Reader*, 120, states: "Marcos's communiqués are available in at least 14 languages."

147   In his "A History of Challenging Messages," *envío*, no. 418, May 2016, http://www.envio.org.ni/articulo/5188.

148   They are: Thomas Olesen, *International Zapatismo: The Construction of Solidarity in the Age of Globalization* (London: Zed Books, 2005); and Alex Khasnabish, *Zapatismo Beyond Borders: New Imaginations of Political Possibility* (Toronto: University of Toronto Press, 2008). In Spanish, see too Guiomar Rovira, *Zapatistas sin fronteras* (Mexico City: Ediciones Era, 2009).

149   In his *International Zapatismo*, 11–13.

150   Interview with Ann Louise Bardach, "Mexico's Poet Rebel," 132; and interview with Medea Benjamin, "Interview: Subcomandante Marcos," *First World*, 67.

151   *Zapatismo Beyond Borders*, 276 and 133, respectively.

152   *Zapatismo Beyond Borders*, 26–27.

153   *International Zapatismo*, 10, and *Zapatismo Beyond Borders*, 278, respectively.

154   Khasnabish, *Zapatistas: Rebellion*, 169 and 178; and Olesen, *International Zapatismo*, 108, 111, and 136.

155 Quoted in Fernanda Navarro, "Vive la Crise!," in Nick Nesbitt ed., *The Concept in Crisis*, 287.

156 In Subcomandante Marcos, *The Zapatistas' Dignified Rage*, 121.

157 See Marcos' December 2007 presentation: "The EZLN is an organization that has flatly refused to hegemonize and homogenize its relationships with other groups, collectives, organizations, peoples, and individuals.... It is not nor has it been the EZLN's objective to create a movement under its hegemony, homogenized with its times, ways, and *no ways*." (In Subcomandante Marcos, *The Zapatistas' Dignified Rage*, 85 and 86.)

158 In "Mayan Zapatista Movement," in *The Legacy of Mesoamerica*, 2nd edn., eds. Robert M. Carmack, Janine L. Gasco, and Gary H. Gossen (Oxford: Routledge, 2007), 381.

159 "The Unknown Icon," 122.

160 See, respectively: Michal Osterweil, "The Italian anomaly: Place and History in the Global Justice Movement," *Understanding European Movements: New Social Movements, Global Justice Struggles, Anti-Austerity Protest*, eds. Cristina Flesher Fominaya and Laurence Cox (London: Routledge, 2013), 42–43; Andrea Membretti and Pierpaolo Mudu, "Where Global Meets Local: Italian Social Centres and the Alterglobalization Movement," *Understanding European Movements*, 86; and Michael Hardt and Antonio Negri, *Multitude: War and Democracy in the Age of Empire* (New York: Penguin, 2004), 266.

161 For more on this collective's foundation, mission, and activities, see its webpage: https://chtodelat.org/. This quotation can be found at: https://bit.ly/2TFQfvH.

162 Khasnabish, *Zapatismo Beyond Borders*, 10–11.

163 See Khasnabish, *Zapatismo Beyond Borders*, 12–14.

164 Khasnabish, *Zapatistas: Rebellion*, 187–188.

165 In his interview with Critical-Theory.com; posted online at: https://bit.ly/2Jln2RO.

166 In Subcomandante Marcos, *Our Word*, 117.

[167] See above, p. 131, n. 1, for my choice of the term "alter-globalisation" as opposed to that of "anti-globalisation" which is employed by others quoted below.

[168] Paul Kingsnorth, *One No, Many Yeses* (London: Simon & Schuster, 2003), 36 and 37.

[169] See Kingsnorth, *One No, Many Yeses*, 73; and the PGA's "hallmarks" as listed on its Wikipedia entry (https://bit.ly/2UKugAk).

[170] Kingsnorth, *One No, Many Yeses*, 73–74. Similarly, see also Khasnabish, *Zapatistas: Rebellion*, 180.

[171] In his "Forward Dreaming: Zapatismo and the Radical Imagination," in *The Movements of Movements*, 590.

[172] *The Sixth Declaration of the Lacandon Jungle* (June 2005), my translation. A slightly different translation can be found in Subcomandante Marcos, *The Speed of Dreams*, 282–283. Interestingly, one of Marcos' first mentions of "another politics" appears in a communiqué dating October 2, 1998, entitled "Tlatelolco: Thirty Years Later the Struggle Continues," which was addressed "To the Generation of Dignity of 1968," and paid tribute to the left-wing activists of old (in Subcomandante Marcos, *Our Word*, 151).

[173] In his interview with Aura Bogado (March 10, 2006), posted online at: https://bit.ly/2CoCSoR.

[174] In García Márquez, "The Punch Card and the Hour Glass," 70 and 71.

[175] In Alma Guillermoprieto, *Looking for History*, 202.

[176] In Subcomandante Marcos, *Our Word*, 228.

[177] Elsewhere, in a 2003 communiqué, Marcos puts it more starkly, stating: "I shit on all the revolutionary vanguards of this planet"; posted online at: https://bit.ly/2FikvUA.

[178] Quoted by Régis Debray, "A Guerrilla with a Difference," in *The Zapatista Reader*, 349–350.

[179] My translation. The text of the original, Spanish version of this speech can be found online at: https://bit.ly/2HrjmfF.

180 In Gloria Muñoz Ramírez, *The Fire and the Word: A History of the Zapatista Movement* (San Francisco: City Lights Publishers, 2008), 305 and 307.

181 In Subcomandante Marcos, *Our Word*, 440.

182 Commentary No. 224 (January 1, 2008), "What Have the Zapatistas Accomplished?", posted online at http://www.binghamton.edu/fbc/archive/224en.htm.

183 In Subcomandante Marcos, *The Zapatistas' Dignified Rage*, 84.

184 In "The Punch Card and the Hour Glass," 71.

185 In Subcomandante Marcos, *The Zapatistas' Dignified Rage*, 181.

186 In Subcomandante Marcos, *Our Word*, 440.

187 Marcos, quoted in Ignacio Ramonet, "Marcos marche sur Mexico," *Monde Diplomatique*, March 2001, 17.

188 In Subcomandante Marcos, *¡Ya Basta!*, 163.

189 Marcos, in Jesús Quintero, *Entrevista* (Madrid: Aguilar, 2007), 86 (my translation).

190 In his interview with *Radio El Espectador de Uruguay* (March 15, 2001), https://bit.ly/2F7k6CX (my translation).

191 In Subcomandante Marcos, *¡Ya Basta!*, 163.

192 Numerous notable examples of these are provided in Tyler Bridges, "From Guerrillas to Politicians," *The Miami Herald*, January 22, 2006, https://bit.ly/2HEvKIE.

193 Marcos' most vehemently and explicitly anti-capitalist works include: "The Fourth World War Has Begun" (August 1997), which is alternatively titled "Seven Loose Pieces of The Global Jigsaw Puzzle"; "The Fourth World War" (November 1999); "The (Impossible) Geometry of Power" (2005); "Zapatistas and the Other: The Pedestrians of History" (2006); and the Subcomandante's presentations contained in EZLN, *Critical Thought in the Face of the Capitalist Hydra* and Subcomandante Marcos, *The Zapatistas' Dignified Rage*. His "The Genealogy of the Crime" (in EZLN, *Critical Thought*, 237–256) is most obviously and explicitly indebted to Marx's *Capital*, but see also pages 226, 245, 267, and 269 of the same book.

194 See, notably, though not only, Subcomandante Marcos, *The Zapatistas' Dignified Rage*, 51 and 101–102.

195 The first two quotations are from Subcomandante Marcos, *The Zapatistas' Dignified Rage*, 63; the third one is from EZLN, *Critical Thought*, 239.

196 In Subcomandante Marcos, *The Zapatistas' Dignified Rage*, 87, 84, and 52, respectively.

197 In EZLN, *Critical Thought*, 239.

198 "Words of the EZLN on the 22nd Anniversary of the Beginning of the War against Oblivion," Enlace Zapatista, January 1, 2016, https://bit.ly/2F8XlyD.

199 Subcomandante Marcos, "The Fourth World War Has Begun," (translated by Nathalie de Broglio), *Nepantla: Views from South* 2, no. 3 (2001), 569.

200 Marcos, *The Zapatistas' Dignified Rage*, 78–79 and 82.

201 See Subcomandante Marcos, *The Zapatistas' Dignified Rage*, 125 and 128; and Marcos' communiqué titled "Them and Us. VII: The Smallest of the Small"; accessible at: https://bit.ly/2UHMke3.

202 Zapatista territory is said to have a population of approximately 300,000 mostly indigenous people, and is organized into five zones consisting of roughly forty municipalities each of which contains numerous local communities. (See Alvaro Reyes and Mara Kaufman, "Sovereignty, Indigeneity, Territory: Zapatista Autonomy and the New Practices of Decolonization," *The South Atlantic Quarterly* 110, no. 2 (2011), 516.)

203 Alvaro Reyes and Mara Kaufman, "Sovereignty, Indigeneity, Territory," 505–525.

204 In Subcomandante Marcos, *The Zapatistas' Dignified Rage*, 160. On the relative successes and achievements of Zapatista autonomous communities regarding providing access to justice, education, and healthcare, especially compared to those living in non-Zapatista communities in Chiapas, see Reyes and Kaufman, "Sovereignty, Indigeneity, Territory," 520–521.

205 Alvaro Reyes, 'The Zapatista Challenge: Politics After Catastrophe," *Cultural Dynamics* 28, no. 2 (2016), 163.

206 Richard Stahler-Sholk, "Constructing Autonomy: Zapatista Strategies of Indigenous Resistance in Mexico," in *The New Global Politics: Global Social Movement in the Twenty-First Century*, eds. Harry E. Vanden, Peter N. Funke, and Gary Prevost (London: Routledge, 2017), 14.

207 "The Zapatista Challenge," 164.

208 Guillermo Gómez-Peña, *Dangerous Border Crossers: The Artist Talks Back* (London: Routledge, 2000), 224.

209 See Brian Gollnick, *Reinventing the Lacandón: Subaltern Representations in the Rain Forest of Chiapas* (Tucson: University of Arizona Press, 2008), 155: "Subcomandante Marcos has done more than any other individual in the last decade to alter the discourse and iconography of the global left."

210 In Marcos, *The Zapatistas' Dignified Rage*, 115.

211 Quoted and translated in Nick Henck, *Insurgent Marcos*, 264.

212 See Paul Kingsnorth, *One No, Many Yeses*, 27: "Every political movement needs its icon and Marcos, whether he likes it or not, has become one – not simply for the Zapatistas of Chiapas, but also for the growing global movement they helped to spawn."

213 Andrew Jones, *Globalization: Key Thinkers* (Cambridge: Polity, 2010), 181.

214 See Marcos' interview with Julio Scherer, "La entrevista insólita," *Proceso* no. 1271, March 11, 2001, 14–15. The magazine's front cover displays a photograph of the two men talking with the quotation "Soy rebelde, no revolucionario ['I am a rebel, not a revolutionary']" as its headline.

215 In Tom Hayden ed., *The Zapatista Reader*, 123.

216 In his, "El Che, desde el fondo de su noche," *El País*, October 9, 1997, https://bit.ly/2Jg3huW.

217 I am writing this on April 3, 2018, a day which saw three high-profile former presidents from three different continents either facing corruption charges in court, being sentenced for them by a court, or appealing against having already been convicted of them by a court (respectively: Jacob Zuma of South Africa, Park Geun-hye of South Korea, and Luiz Inácio Lula da Silva of Brazil).

218 See Andrew Reding and Christopher Whalen, "NAFTA and Mexico: The Perfect Dictatorship: Repression and One-Party Rule in Mexico," *Multinational Monitor*, 1993, https://bit.ly/2HpJ8Rp. They cite physical intimidation of and violent attacks (including murder) on journalists by police, and write that:

> More than 100 members of the center-left Party of the Democratic Revolution (PRD) have been killed by security forces, goon squads and PRI members since the 1988 presidential election. PRD mayors have been shot at, detained on trumped-up charges of drug dealing and terrorism, tortured and imprisoned.

On the failure of "...the Salinas government...[to] reverse... Mexico's long-standing policy of impunity for those who commit human rights abuses," which includes "[t]he use of torture by federal and state police," see the 1992 *Human Rights Watch World Report: Mexico*, accessible at: https://bit.ly/2JgX16h. Finally, see Nick Henck, *Subcommander Marcos*, 60-61, 121–122, 125, and 139, for human rights abuses, including state repression, in Chiapas, under State Governor Patrocinio González Garrido (1988–1993), Salinas' cousin by marriage.

TIERRA
Y
LIBERTAD

LAND&
LIBERTY

ANARCHIST INFLUENCES IN THE
MEXICAN REVOLUTION
RICARDO FLORES
MAGON

The Other Mexico

The North American Triangle Completed

John Warnock

YOUR FREEDOM AND MINE

Abdullah Öcalan and
the Kurdish Question
in Erdoğan's Turkey

Edited by
Thomas Jeffrey Miley
and Federico Venturini

Foreword by Dilar Dirik

BLACK ROSE BOOKS

Filtering the News

Essays on Herman and Chomsky's Propaganda Model

Jeffery Klaehn, editor

THE ESSENCE
OF CAPITALISM

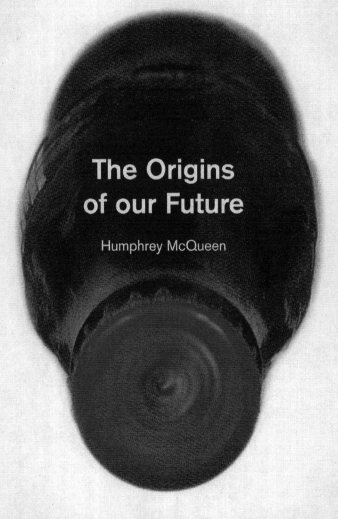

The Origins
of our Future

Humphrey McQueen

POLITICAL ECOLOGY
SYSTEM CHANGE NOT CLIMATE CHANGE

DIMITRIOS
ROUSSOPOULOS

BLACK
ROSE
BOOKS